Buying for
Business

Buying for Business

Insights in purchasing and supply management

Christopher Barrat
and
Mark Whitehead

WILEY

Other Wiley Editorial Offices

John Wiley & Sons Inc., 111 River Street, Hoboken, NJ 07030, USA

Jossey-Bass, 989 Market Street, San Francisco, CA 94103-1741, USA

Wiley-VCH Verlag GmbH, Boschstr. 12, D-69469 Weinheim, Germany

John Wiley & Sons Australia Ltd, 33 Park Road, Milton, Queensland 4064, Australia

John Wiley & Sons (Asia) Pte Ltd, 2 Clementi Loop #02-01, Jin Xing Distripark, Singapore 129809

John Wiley & Sons Canada Ltd, 22 Worcester Road, Etobicoke, Ontario, Canada M9W 1L1

Wiley also publishes its books in a variety of electronic formats. Some content that appears in print may
not be available in electronic books.

British Library Cataloguing in Publication Data

A catalogue record for this book is available from the British Library

ISBN 0-470-09246-7

Typeset by Dobbie Typesetting Ltd, Tavistock, Devon
Printed and bound in Great Britain by T.J. International, Padstow, Cornwall
This book is printed on acid-free paper responsibly manufactured from sustainable forestry in which at
least two trees are planted for each one used for paper production.

Contents

Preface and Acknowledgements

Why this book is for you

I F YOU HAVE AN INTEREST IN PURCHASING AND SUPPLY MANAGEMENT, *Buying for Business* will tell you something of what it involves in an interesting and helpful way.

The business function variously called purchasing, procurement and supply management covers a wide area. At one end are the practical questions – how to write a contract and negotiate a good deal, for example – while at the other end are ethical issues about sourcing cheap goods from developing countries.

Nevertheless, it's an area that has received relatively little focused attention in the business world. This book is aimed at helping remedy that deficiency. It is not meant to be a manual of purchasing techniques or an academic textbook. Instead, we hope it's an interesting, even challenging read, airing some of the issues associated with this area of business.

Anyone wanting to know more about purchasing and supply management will find *Buying for Business* useful. Students of the subject, people new to a job in this field and managers needing to know what their colleagues down the corridor in purchasing get up to should all have a copy to hand. Some of the ideas we present will interest academics and consultants. Decision makers in government will also find it a useful introduction to an increasingly important area.

And in case the title may mislead, *Buying for Business* is not aimed solely at the private sector. Far from it: purchasing and supply management are equally important in the public and voluntary sectors. The book is meant for everyone with an interest in the subject across all sectors.

How to read this book

The best way to read this book is probably while sitting on a balcony overlooking the Mediterranean with a cool drink in hand. *Buying for Business* is written so that it can be read as a complete text from start to finish, but it also lends itself to dipping into. So if you have 20 minutes in an airport lounge or want to brush up on e-commerce before your meeting with the MD, you can simply take a single chapter at a time.

The book starts with a chapter outlining the scope of the subject and then goes in more detail into the practical side of purchasing and supply management in Chapters 2, 3, 4 and 5. Chapters 6–11 cover some of the bigger issues that often arise in discussions among purchasing professionals. The final chapter offers some ideas on what the future may hold for purchasers.

We didn't intend to cover everything and we have presented our own take on the issues involved. It is our wish that *Buying for Business* will help raise the status of the purchasing and supply management profession and shed light on the debates that are sometimes over-complicated.

Above all, we want it to stimulate discussion. Purchasing and supply management is still a young profession and there's much to be sorted out. We hope that *Buying for Business* will help with that process.

Acknowledgements

We would like to thank the following for their help in providing valuable feedback while *Buying for Business* was being planned and written: Guy Allan, Abbey; Robin Cammish, QP Group; Andrew Cox, the Centre for Business Strategy and Procurement, Birmingham Business School; Chris Gallagher, CIPS; John Hatton, Trading Partners; Melinda Johnson, IdEA; Richard Lamming, Southampton Business School; Douglas MacKellar, Supply Side Focus; Peter Marson, 4C Associates; Carolyn Munton, CIPS; David Rich-Jones, Xchanging; Peter Smith, Procurement Excellence; Mark Williams, Supply Chain Personnel; Neil Weaver, PZ Cussons; Bill Young.

Christopher Barrat and Mark Whitehead

1
Everyone's a Buyer . . .

W E ALL LIKE TO GO TO THE SHOPS AND SPEND NOW AND THEN, in fact every day most of us spend money one way or another. So we must be quite good at it.

It's the same at work. Most people spend their company's money from time to time. Nearly everyone likes to have a say in how money is spent on their behalf. In most organizations people at all levels are involved in one way or another with buying anything from paperclips to computers.

It's not difficult to pick up the phone to a company you deal with and put in an order, or to log on to a travel site on the Internet and book your own flights. Nowadays, it's not too much of an exaggeration to say that everyone's a buyer . . .

. . . but not an expert buyer

While most people like to spend their employer's cash, very often they are not actually achieving real value for money. This means that a lot of the money being spent by organizations of all kinds, from small businesses to local authorities to big companies, is wasted.

However, many companies employ specialists to spend money in an efficient, well-organized way. These purchasing professionals have the training, experience and market knowledge to make a better job of it. They are not necessarily the only ones who can do the purchasing and look after suppliers, but they are the experts. Their skills, ideally, will be highly sought-after. Everyone should want to involve them in their purchasing decisions because of the benefits they offer.

The hidden bonanza

There are big prizes to be won. Every organization wants to make more money, or at least to make sure that its limited resources are deployed effectively. The obvious way for a commercial organization to increase profitability is to raise prices, or sell more, or both. As Figure 1.1 illustrates, while fixed and variable costs will probably rise too, the profit margin is likely to grow faster.

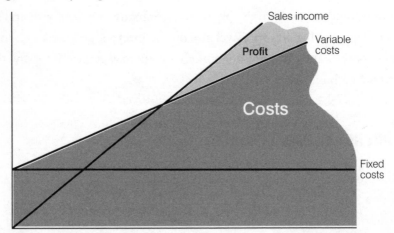

Figure 1.1

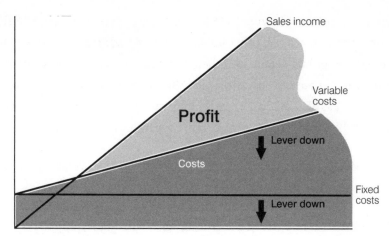

Figure 1.2

However, businesses are realizing that another way of becoming more profitable can be just as effective, if not more so – improving the purchasing operation. As Figure 1.2 shows, driving down variable and fixed costs through effective purchasing is just as effective in increasing profits as improving sales figures. And, as we shall see, concentrating on the purchasing function may also bring other benefits.

Undiscovered territory

Progress towards reforming purchasing functions is uneven. Many big, established companies have reformed their procurement, although often this merely reveals how much there is to do before they will become truly efficient. It's among small and medium-sized enterprises that purchasing remains largely unorganized and inefficient.

In the public sector, reform of purchasing is now high on the political agenda. The government has realized just how much can be saved through streamlining buying by Whitehall departments, local authorities, the NHS, universities and other public bodies. At the time of writing, huge savings in the public sector were being discussed, based largely on greater centralization of buying operations and the adoption of e-procurement. The government has also made it clear that big increases in NHS spending must be effectively controlled to ensure value for money.

The surprising fact is that most organizations in the private, public and voluntary sectors simply don't know:

1. How much money they're spending with third-party suppliers.
2. Who's spending it.
3. What they're getting for their money.

This is partly because many people in business, often running large, well-known organizations, prefer to concentrate on more glamorous activities: sales, marketing and advertising, for example. Or finance, where the real decisions affecting the bottom line are made, or HR, where the huge amounts spent on the most important assets for any organization – its people – are controlled.

These functions attract enormous interest in the commercial and academic world. Go into any bookshop and look at the business section: there is likely to be a large selection of titles on marketing, selling and, quite likely, advertising. Look at the shelves filled with books on finance. And you won't be able to miss the huge numbers of 'inspirational' books by big-name management gurus offering recipes for instant commercial success, often focusing on sales and people management.

In contrast, there will be few books on purchasing and supply management. In most bookshops there are likely to be no more than a couple of academic and highly technical tomes. Some general management books will probably contain references to purchasing or certain subsections of the field, inventory management, for example.

Click on to the website of any major business school and search for 'marketing' or 'advertising' and there will be a plethora of courses specializing in these subjects. Now look for 'purchasing' or 'supply management' and you might discover a module or two buried in another more general course.

Examine the structure of contemporary companies and you will almost certainly find marketing and sales as separate functions, most likely with a representative at board level. Purchasing and supply management, though, are probably lurking within the manufacturing or finance department, or as part of central administration or some other branch of the company structure. Representation at board level is rare.

What is purchasing and supply management?

As a relatively young area of activity, many people are unclear what purchasing and supply management involves. This is almost certainly one reason for its relative obscurity on the business scene.

Roles within these functions vary enormously and the definitions are often somewhat hazy. But essentially, anyone who is involved in buying goods or services on behalf of their organization, arranging their delivery and monitoring their cost and effectiveness, can fall within the definition of a purchasing or supply management professional.

This extends from the junior buyer in a small or medium-sized company right up to the procurement director of a major multinational. Purchasing and supply management professionals can be found in all sectors of industry and commerce, and in the public and voluntary sectors. Organizations ranging from small companies to major multinationals and from town halls to government departments are all quite likely to employ people responsible for buying goods and services.

It's estimated that in the UK there are perhaps 150 000 people working in purchasing and supply management roles. If the wider field of logistics is also included – people concerned with the movement of goods rather than specifically with their purchase – the number of professionals involved could be 250 000.

In the smallest enterprises, a separate role for a purchasing specialist may not have emerged: the managing director or finance director or one of the partners may do the buying. Or quite likely, everyone chips in as necessary.

But as with other functions, once an organization reaches a certain size, specialism tends to become necessary for efficiency and someone is likely to be tasked with managing purchasing.

A typical SME with a few hundred staff might have a purchasing department of two or three people. In the biggest companies, purchasing departments often comprise several dozen people responsible for different aspects of the buying and supply management operation.

Raising the profile

Purchasing has traditionally been a low-profile function. Very often it has been the department where people deal with the administration surrounding purchases: signing invoices and matching them to purchase orders, answering enquiries from suppliers and keeping records.

It has often been an unglamorous, bread-and-butter department where life passes uneventfully. In this kind of scenario, the department's boss doesn't wield much influence with the higher-ups and is unlikely to be involved in discussions about the organization's strategy. The board doesn't pay much heed to what purchasing is up to because it isn't considered very important.

While it's still like this in many organizations, it is changing. In the past ten or twenty years many companies have taken the first steps towards giving purchasing and supply management the attention it deserves. In part, circumstances have forced the change. Increasing competition and a difficult economic climate have led companies to look for ways of becoming ever more efficient.

In the 1980s 'downsizing' was the order of the day, when companies cut costs by reducing the number of staff on their payroll. This had the advantage of being quick and effective, but as many organizations later realized, the danger is that expertise gained by individuals over many years is thrown out and proves impossible to replace when it is needed again.

The ability to squeeze costs by cutting numbers is limited, so many organizations looked for other ways to become more competitive. Some realized that there was money to be saved from the huge amounts spent on goods and services. They saw that reducing purchasing costs could improve profitability – often dramatically. In the case of public-sector organizations such as schools or the health services, this means that the money saved can be diverted to paying for what really matters: the front-line services of teaching children or treating the sick.

The new interest in the purchasing function has continued to grow as reform of spending operations in companies and public bodies has steadily produced results. Purchasing has been given a new lease of life and those involved in it are gaining status, not only in their own organizations but also in the wider business world.

It is a trend that seems certain to continue. In 1997, according to research by business analysts Gartner in the US, very few chief executive officers would have even known the name of their senior procurement professional. But 'the recent intense interest in procurement means that senior executives across all industry sectors are beginning to realize the true potential of procurement'.

By 2007, Gartner says, at least half of the biggest global companies will have a chief procurement officer reporting directly to the CEO.

What do purchasing people do?

As we have said, everyone is in some sense a buyer, but many organizations are now appointing specialist purchasing professionals. Nevertheless, there is a long way to go in most organizations before purchasing becomes a highly developed function on a par with sales, finance, marketing or HR.

The potential for change in many companies and public-sector organizations is thus huge. But the study of purchasing and supply management as a business function is still in its infancy and for most people it is difficult to know where to start.

Much of the research into purchasing and supply chain theory so far has been concerned with mapping out what is involved in it. Unlike more developed functions, people studying this still often ask themselves: 'What do purchasing and supply management professionals actually do?'

A major study due to be completed in 2004 will attempt to answer this question. The four professional institutes whose members work in purchasing, supply management and logistics have joined forces to analyse the skills needed by people in more than 50 identified roles.

The findings of the Polemics project will be used to make sure that professional qualifications are more relevant to industry as part of a government drive to raise skills levels in the UK workforce.

Information is key

The basic ideas involved in professional purchasing and supply management are fairly simple. There is no need to grapple with complex statistical formulas or difficult management concepts, though these have their place. More important is to understand the ideas involved. Once you can see where you're going, the means of getting there will become clearer. As psychologist Kurt Lewin once said: 'There's nothing so practical as a good theory.'

Often the basic information needed to make real changes is lacking, because historically very little attention has been paid to the way in which purchasing is organized and what it does. Consequently, there is often a complex web of purchasing activities in most organizations that is very difficult to analyse, and even more difficult to organize into a rational and controllable function.

That means that purchasing and supply management consultants – a growing breed of experts – spend a great deal of time grappling with questions about who is spending money in organizations, how much they are spending, who they are spending it with and whether they are getting good value.

Supply chains

Terminology is often a stumbling block when trying to understand the issues involved in purchasing. 'Supply chain', for example, is one of the expressions commonly used to describe a concept of which most people in purchasing will have heard. It's important that they should understand what it means, because they are part of it, and if they feel they are involved in something more important than merely placing the next order, it will help develop an understanding of the bigger picture. For many purchasers, seeing themselves as crucial players in the economy as a whole will be highly motivating.

The idea of a supply chain is based on the concept of a string of organizations along which items are passed while in the process of being developed. A manufacturing company will typically buy raw materials – metals, plastics or other commodities, for example – and transform them into an item that may then go on to the next link in the chain. The next company in the chain will carry out further processes before the item finally ends up being sold as a product in the shops and supermarkets.

In the motor-manufacturing sector, for example, several thousands of suppliers are typically linked together to contribute to the finished product that ends up in the car showroom.

This basic understanding applies just as much in the services sector, even though the product on sale is not a tangible object. IT services, for example, often involve highly paid teams of people installing expensive machinery or providing business advice. These activities are probably a crucial aspect of the company's operation and a high-cost one at that. If a company is selling IT services, it is a supplier and is therefore, it can be argued, part of a supply chain.

However, many experts now question the concept of the supply chain, pointing out that in reality the links between organizations are far more complex than the term suggests. They often look not so much like a chain as, for example, a network of many organizations linked to one another in different ways. So they argue that 'supply networks' is a more accurate way of describing these relationships than 'supply chains'. These are simply ways of understanding how things work.

Who is spending money?

One of the first tasks to address if you want to bring your purchasing/ supply management function under control is to find out who is spending money. This may sound like a very simple question, but for most organizations it is a very difficult one to answer.

There are usually a few people whose roles may clearly involve purchasing, at least from time to time. IT managers typically deal directly with contractors and suppliers and often manage very big spending budgets. The HR department may make its own decisions about spending on goods and services ranging from software to writing projects. Engineers have traditionally bought their own goods as they are the ones who know what to buy.

However, in most organizations there will be many other people who spend money. Most of the spending will be 'historical' – no one knows when it was decided that they would take responsibility for their purchasing. It seems as if it has always been done that way.

Often there will be others who spend money from time to time even though this has never been officially sanctioned. 'Maverick spending', as this is known, is the bugbear of the professional purchaser. Although it can often amount to quite large amounts of money, it is completely unmonitored and uncontrolled.

Increasing value through purchasing

Cost: The quick fix

Of the various ways in which improving an organization's purchasing and supply management function can bring benefits, the most obvious is cost reduction. As we saw early in this chapter, reducing fixed and variable costs through effective purchasing strategies can help increase profits. Furthermore, it can be argued, the savings available through a more efficient purchasing operation can be of far more immediate benefit than raised income from sales.

The argument goes like this: Suppose some smart purchaser realizes that the price being paid for widgets can be cut by 20%. Instead of spending

£100 000 a year on this particular type of widget, the company can source the same item from another supplier for £80 000.

The £20 000 saved has an immediate impact on the company's relative profits – it goes 'straight to the bottom line'. Or it can be reinvested to improve the quality of the product or to reduce its price in the marketplace, thus sharpening the company's competitive edge. In the case of public- and voluntary-sector organizations, the money saved can be used to improve services.

To achieve the same benefits through increased sales would mean a huge increase in volumes sold. If profits average, for example, 20% of sales income, each £100 000 of sales would generate £20 000 of profit. So to create the same £20 000 extra profit, our imaginary company would have to double its sales.

There are two main areas in which purchasing costs can be cut: spending with suppliers and transaction costs.

Cutting spending with suppliers can mean, for example, securing lower prices by aggregation: putting all the orders for an item, previously perhaps generated in different parts of the organization, together into one big order, and negotiating discounts based on volume.

Or it may be possible simply to find suppliers who offer a better deal. The incumbent may be inefficient and offer poor value for money; researching the market to identify whether other suppliers can give a better deal is a fundamental part of the purchaser's job.

It may also be possible to negotiate a better deal with the existing supplier, especially if the purchaser is armed with information about other companies offering better deals. It is considered good practice regularly to 'benchmark' suppliers against their peers – taking prices and other factors such as reliability into account – to make sure that they remain good value for money.

The other major way of saving through purchasing is to reduce what are known as 'transaction costs'. These are the costs of the transaction involved in making a purchase, not including the amount of money paid for the item. How this is measured is open to interpretation, but should ideally incorporate everything, including the cost of running the purchasing department. So the transaction cost involved in a single purchase can be worked out by dividing the total cost of a purchasing operation by the number of transactions it handles. It follows that transaction costs can be cut by reducing the costs involved in running the purchasing operation.

Quality

Professional purchasing is not merely about cutting costs, important though that is in today's competitive world. In a slightly less immediate and direct way, a properly run purchasing department can bring huge benefits to a company by improving the quality of its product.

Consider cookery. The first rule of good cookery is to use the best ingredients. No amount of culinary expertise can cover up for substandard raw materials. You can't, as the saying goes, make a silk purse out of a sow's ear. The same applies to any product in the world of industry and commerce. As the person who knows what is available on the market, how to get hold of it and how much to pay for it, the purchaser is in the best position to make sure that the best ingredients are being bought.

It is possible, of course, to go for the lowest price at all times. Quality generally costs more. So there is a balance to be reached between cost and quality: as a generalization, the more you pay, the higher-quality goods or services you are likely to receive.

But that is the simplest way of looking at it and, as everyone knows, paying more does not necessarily mean getting better value. In reality the world is more complicated. It's the professional purchaser's job to make sense of the complex issues involved and come up with the best possible deal in terms of both cost and quality. The big question is how to achieve maximum cost-effectiveness.

Optimum cost-effectiveness will depend on several factors, including what use the bought-in item is going to be put to and how crucial it is in the production process. The decision on cost-effectiveness may also be affected by how much money is available to spend. It would make no sense for a purchaser to insist on buying the very best available on the market if the company can't afford to pay the bill.

There is also the question of how important the purchaser's employer believes quality to be. Or, to put it in a more practical way, whether the company's customer is paying for top-quality goods or is happy to make do with lower standards.

A factor gaining increasing recognition as one that can bring huge benefits to an organisation in the marketplace is the innovation that suppliers can bring. Suppliers are generally in competition with one another and the way they gain competitive edge, apart from factors such as price and reliability, is through offering better goods or services than their rivals. Innovation is a key driver for suppliers and an astute purchaser will take full advantage of this.

Reputation

An even bigger issue in which the professional purchaser is often involved is how relationships with suppliers can affect an organization's performance in the longer term. One increasingly crucial factor in this concerns image and reputation.

Nowadays there are much more complex and longer-term questions to consider than the simple cost of an item or its specification. What organizations buy and where they buy it from can also affect far more than immediate profitability.

No organization wants to hit the headlines because one of its suppliers exploits children in the developing world or is destroying a wildlife haven. Most organizations want to be thought of as dynamic and commercially minded, but they also want to be seen as responsible. This is not just a noble aspiration but good business sense.

Increasing long-term value

The various ways of increasing value through purchasing can be seen as a progression in which an organization can become increasingly sophisticated. As purchasing skills and experience develop, it can move from a strategy of implementing the simplest way of boosting immediate short-term value – cutting costs – through increasingly higher-level activities bringing longer-term value. Figure 1.3 shows the progression from cost cutting to improving reputation and the consequent rise in an organization's long-term value.

The prize

There is therefore huge scope in almost every organization for examining exactly what is being bought and whether it provides value for money. One of the winners in last year's CIPS/Supply Management awards was the Pennine Acute Hospitals NHS Trust. This example shows how effective purchasing can make a real difference.

The trust's supplies manager, David Scott, who also won an individual award, discovered that endoscopy equipment, used in internal examinations, had been bought from the same supplier for 27 years without ever being put out to tender. So Scott put the items out to tender and ended up buying 12 new endoscopes at a saving of 33%. One examination room was completely refitted and a total saving of £140 000 was secured over the seven-year life cycle of the product.

Scott spread the word and several other NHS trusts took advantage of the same deal. It is now being extended to trusts nationwide at a projected saving to the NHS of £15 million a year.

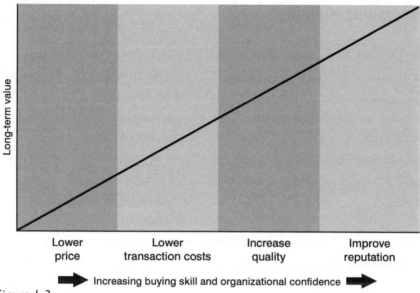

| Lower price | Lower transaction costs | Increase quality | Improve reputation |

Increasing buying skill and organizational confidence

Figure 1.3

One of the judges for the awards said that this was 'an excellent example of one purchasing department challenging the status quo and stimulating a change in attitudes throughout the public sector'. He added that it was 'the best thing that has happened in health service purchasing for a long time'.

The new equipment was not only much cheaper but also more reliable, easier to maintain and less uncomfortable for the patient being examined. Everyone was a winner – except the original supplier who failed to keep up with technological developments and, in the end, lost out.

This was just one piece of equipment found in any general hospital. The savings that could theoretically be made if the same approach were applied to all health service spending are incalculable.

Concluding thoughts

The purchasing function plays a crucial role in most organizations, yet many still haven't recognized its importance. How many of us would take such a casual attitude to buying a house or car?

Companies usually spend large amounts of money on bought-in goods and services. Yet many don't know who is spending that money, how much they're spending, or who they're spending it with. They are like charitable institutions keeping inefficient suppliers in business.

The savings that can be achieved from streamlining purchasing are huge. Nevertheless, many organizations still haven't got round to looking at it closely. Shareholders, customers and the public would soon start asking questions if they realized how much money was being wasted.

It's clear that purchasing as a function ought to have a voice on the board of management in most organizations, but this is very rare. How can purchasing professionals start fighting their way to the top?

Most professions have their stars – people who are recognized as being excellent at what they do and an example to all, as well as first-class communicators who know how to use the media. Yet it's hard to name any such gurus in the world of purchasing and supply management. It's time for a few ambitious individuals to step into the limelight.

2
Managing Purchasing People

THE STRATEGIC IMPORTANCE OF SUPPLY SIDE MANAGEMENT IS trumpeted by many a publication. Many purchasing groups want to be considered important forces in the business – which we saw in Chapter 1 they should be. Purchasing can occupy this position. It can be a stimulating catalyst for development and diversification. It can be modern in its management approach and be seen not only as a department that makes things happen, but also as a 'place to be'.

On the other hand, it can easily occupy the tawdry end of the business, with the processing efficiency of an EU committee and the cooperative capability of football fans. It can be seen as administrative, obstructive and bureaucratic. It can be staffed by the sort of people who wanted to be commercial but never really made it. It can be seen as the department that stops things happening, and a 'place to avoid'.

There are examples of purchasing groups at both ends of this spectrum. This chapter will look at how to manage and motivate purchasing people.

It will look at how to get the best from them and help them to develop. All of this can determine whether purchasing is a sad or sexy place to be.

The purchasing person

In the world of modern management methods you're in danger of being burned at the stake if you stereotype particular groups. All marketers are schmoozers, sales people are slimy, accountants are dull, IT people are geeks and so on. However, for the purposes of managing purchasing it can be useful to have an idea of what purchasers are like. Understanding their key characteristics may help with managing them effectively.

Nature and nurture

In general, a firm of forensic accounts auditors is likely to be staffed with people who have a strong attention to detail, an investigative mind and a numerical bias. Broadly speaking sales people will want to look forward, have great breadth but little depth and won't be great completer-finishers. The nature of these different jobs will attract people of a certain type – there is a pre-selection effect. In the same way, purchasing will naturally attract a certain type of person.

Once in the role, there will also be a nurturing effect, with certain types of behaviour being reinforced and others dwindling through lack of use. This nature and nurture will over time produce the beast known as the 'typical purchaser'. Here are some broad characteristics that you find in purchasing groups.

Independence

One strong element in purchasing people tends to be independence. At one end of this spectrum you have the helpful concepts of integrity, challenge, objective thought and getting on with the job – the sort of style that can characterize purchasers as hard negotiators. At the other end you will find an attitude type that fluctuates somewhere between belligerence and 'jobsworth'.

Two factors may contribute to this trait. Many purchasers have a technical, engineering or manufacturing background. Many purchasing departments are either aligned to manufacturing or have a heritage there. This makes sense, in that purchasing is a relatively new discipline and the people who need the most buying are in manufacturing.

More recently, purchasing has also been seen as a useful stepping stone for people with technical training to become more commercial. Engineers and R&D folk will often have their first commercial exposure because they need to become involved in a purchasing project.

Technical knowledge is seen as a benefit in some buying roles, where specifications are an important factor in the buying mix. Even in bigger organizations where careers are more structured, it is unusual to find someone moving from manufacturing directly into marketing or sales. But it is common to find them move into purchasing or logistics as an interim step.

The way buyers are regarded by the organization will also strengthen their independence. The vast majority of purchasing groups feel in some way that they are ignored, perhaps undervalued and not involved enough in the business to add the value that they feel they can. If you are ignored long enough, then you tend to become more independent. The effect can lead many purchasers to get on and do the best they can despite their lack of involvement or thanks.

Achievement orientation

Purchasing people get a kick out of seeing things done. This may also be reinforced by the fact that they often get kicked if things are not done.

In marketing, for example, the fuzzy nature of the output can make it hard to pinpoint what has or has not been achieved. In purchasing, if the production line has just ground to a halt because the raw material hopper is empty, then it is all too painfully clear what has not been achieved.

Nobody will thank you on the days the hopper is full, of course. That's a given. And if you don't get many pats on the back for doing your job well, you tend to create your own congratulations – you get pleasure from achievement.

The 'achiever' type of person is pretty self-reliant. They may even resent being thanked, especially when even though there was a good outcome, they realize that it could have been done even more efficiently. There is obviously room for longer-term strategic work in purchasing, but most buying activity involves the short-term completion of tasks: tenders, orders, deliveries, invoices. Purchasing is typical of a job type that will encourage achievers.

Technical bias

This is again closely aligned to the typical heritage of buyers. Visit any buying department and ask how many of the graduates have an arts degree. Or even check how many graduates there are to start with. Although purchasing has in recent years become more popular as an area where graduates want to work, that's a relatively new phenomenon. For a long time new blood came from a combination of R&D, engineering and manufacturing, and this is bound to give it a technical bias. This can be reinforced by the value that the organization places on buyers with long experience.

Professional focus

There are more 'lifers' in purchasing than any other commercial group. It used to be of almost mythical proportions in some areas such as the paints industry. There were plenty of old war-horse buyers, gnarled with experience, by whom fresh-faced reps would be chewed up and spat out.

'Experience' was also seen to be a key advantage in a buyer. In buying groups you often find old-timers whose status is perhaps not revered, but there is certainly a sense of confidence in them. They are seen as 'seasoned professionals' rather than 'sad past-its'.

The changing needs of purchasing

Purchasing used to be simple. You did a bit of haggling once a year, drank the free scotch at Christmas, and then got on with the proper job of placing orders, chasing deliveries and shouting at suppliers.

Then things got all 'strategic'. The challenge is that individuals are being asked to think in this way either without any real development training, or without being able to drop other day-to-day activities.

Buying jobs are unusual in that the more mundane tasks are often carried out by the same person who is doing the sexy bits. A sales person on the road who makes a deal simply sends it through to the office, it's some poor sales administrator who has to get it on the system and persuade logistics to meet the ridiculous delivery schedule.

In purchasing buyers will often enter their own orders, chase delivery, be the focal point for queries, resolve disputes and help reconcile the paperwork. This task diversity is compounded by a new need also to have a wide range of management approaches.

Then along came 'partnering'. Having spent ten happy years beating suppliers with sticks, you suddenly had to ask them to marry you and work together for a golden future. 'Win–win' no longer meant hitting them twice as hard, it meant them getting benefits too. Just as you were getting used to this and even taking them out to lunch, the call came from on high for massive savings and you were back to dusting off your trusty stick – although obviously this time hitting them in the spirit of partnering.

How to manage this change

This combination of skills diversity and strategy changes is a real management issue. Not only does it present simple difficulties of 'skill spread', it can also have more subtle effects, where day-to-day activity is used as a convenient excuse to avoid more strategic work that buyers may feel wary of tackling.

This stretch of roles can be tackled in two simple ways. First, the roles can be reorganized so that more strategic work is put into some jobs and more task-oriented roles are put into another. The other option is to develop purchasing people so that they are appropriately supported to manage the diversity of thinking skills and doing skills.

Both these options have risks. Reorganizing by splitting into more task and strategic roles can leave some people feeling like second-class citizens, with others thinking so strategically that it bears no relation to reality. The development option is dangerous if the assessment of both capability and desire has not been properly made. There is a tendency for managers and staff to believe that everyone wants to take on more strategic and thinking roles. That's not true, and pushing people down this road can at best mean that it simply doesn't get done very well, and at worst can lead to stress.

The biggest danger of all is doing nothing. Purchasing is generally somewhat behind when it comes to developing people, especially around personal and thinking skills. The challenge is therefore either to undertake comprehensive development or, if there is no desire or capability to develop in the group, it is time to bring in new blood.

Motivating a purchasing group

Money

Theorists such as Frederick Herzberg in his 1959 book *The Motivation to Work* listed money as a 'hygiene factor'. People are unhappy if these factors are not present at a basic level. However, once this level is achieved, these factors are not very motivational. He contrasted hygiene factors with real motivators such as personal growth.

Money is therefore something that you need to get right, but don't expect it to be a real motivator. Like working conditions and management rules, if these are poor they can have a demotivating effect, but if they are adequate then they won't actually be motivational. Only when you put a disproportionate prize as the goal do hygiene factors really cause action, and even then it may be for only a few individuals rather than the wider masses.

Money in some form still probably occupies the No. 1 slot for motivational tools used in management, but it is difficult to employ it in purchasing. Commissions work well on relatively small or at least discrete deals, where it was clear that only one person made things happen. Purchasing deals can be ongoing and require many others in the company to make them work. In addition, companies increasingly need to add value. Simply shaving the price is not such an easy option, and added value is harder to measure a monetary value against.

Conditions and status

Herzberg also categorized office conditions as hygiene factors. So giving people a new desk and the office a lick of paint would stop them complaining, but wouldn't actually motivate them.

Purchasing departments are notorious for being 'out the back', stuck somewhere between accounts and production. Some managers have even claimed that purchasing should look run-down in order to justify asking suppliers for discounts.

Ensuring that purchasing staff have appropriate modern conditions and equipment is important, and could have a secondary motivational effect. You will, of course, have to run the gauntlet of jibes from your fellow managers about purchasing 'feathering its own nest'.

Having brushed these aside, it may be that turning your department into a professional place to work will generate feelings of pride. It may also land you better deals. Sales people are sensitive to status and impact. Negotiations conducted by an untidy desk on non-matching chairs in the corner of an open-plan office will be conducted differently from those held in a small but neat office, with modern furniture and space on the walls for a picture of you enjoying a golf day with their main competitors.

Basic job title status is also worth getting right. While adding the title 'manager' to a business card may mean more to 'power-oriented' sales individuals than 'achievement-oriented' purchasing ones, purchasing in general downgrades its staff titles. With sales people increasingly called 'directors' and 'vice-presidents', it is worth checking that your buyers at least have some pride in their own titles.

Organization and structure

Much is made of teamwork as a motivational force. In reality some groups – most notably sales forces – are often not teams at all.

Sales people are individuals with very similar roles, carrying out their jobs as individuals, which is not the same as being in a team. Buying is different. Buyers more often have to interact with different functions – research and development, finance, IT, production – all of whom bring different skills with them. There is also the opportunity in larger companies to bring together buyers from different locations into buying teams or buying streams to work collectively on bigger deals.

As a manager you can use your power and influence to help organize cross-functional teams to form effective buying teams. This brings the purchasing people into the business process at an earlier stage, so that their skills are better understood and more effectively utilized. This is truly motivational.

Portfolio management is another motivational tool that is more easily used in purchasing than in many other functions. The ability to add, swap or exchange a particular category within a buyer's portfolio provides flexibility. On the sales side, you may tinker by adding a few more postcodes to the sales patch, but you can't change half the area without all the upheaval and cost of physically relocating individuals. Likewise in production, if you are located at a smaller site then there may be no other jobs you can do without moving sites. Neither of these restrictions applies to purchasing.

This tool needs to be used with care. Their technical bias and achievement orientation are likely to mean that buyers feel uncertain when faced with a product they are not familiar with. They may take to the new challenge with interest, but they may be wary at first. As a motivational tool, therefore, portfolio management can be effective, but it requires a good deal of management support.

The stimulus of change

Moving people around is a stimulus. It can give them a fresh perspective and help them to shake off problems. The stimulus of change at appropriate levels causes improved or different behaviour, but at too high a level causes stress.

If there are occasional opportunities to move people around the office, therefore, this could be productive. Larger moves, on the other hand, can be difficult. There is a big difference between shuffling a few partitions around the office and relocating a department 240 miles away. In 2003, for example, Nissan looked at relocating a 60-strong purchasing group from the North East of the UK to the Home Counties to put them closer to the engineering development group rather than production, and realize greater savings from earlier and innovative involvement in purchasing projects. The group's dismay at this prospect was so strong that they made moves towards organizing a strike ballot. Not only was strike action pretty much a thing of the past in the car industry, but in Nissan in particular industrial relations were good.

It will always be hard in cases such as this to establish the real savings that could accrue from such a move. With this depth of feeling, the chance of industrial action, resentment towards the potential function they were meant to get closer to and management distraction, the savings must have been vast to justify this sort of play. Big moves of this kind can cause real motivational issues. In this case an actual strike was averted; however, the very fact that it was considered shows that this particular stimulus to change probably crossed over into the realms of real stress.

The best model in practice

Any motivational mechanism can work, and sometimes the most bizarre, or the simplest, proves to be the most effective. Some companies such as Rank Xerox and GE offer major holidays as incentives – for all departments including purchasing. At the simple end of the scale, one senior manager in a chemical company still rates the Buzz Lightyear toy – a gift from his team thanking him for his support – as his most precious reward.

There is a surprisingly straightforward set of criteria that, if followed, guarantees success. Miss any step out, and you are equally assured of failure.

Gate 1: Could I do it?

The individual must believe they can actually do what you are asking them to do. If they really don't think they can, they won't be motivated to try. 'It's all very well you asking me to take a more strategic approach to the supply chain, but what does that really mean?'

This is the classic problem when asking purchasing people to move from transactional to more thinking skills. If they don't think they have the capability, they won't want to do it.

Gate 2: Would it work?

Do they think it will have an effect? If they get the feeling that this is all a passing fad, then why should they bother? 'What is the point in negotiating faster delivery times? We already have warehouses full of finished stock.'

The independence and experience of purchasing people make this a difficult area. They often try hard to make things better, only to find that a lack of preparation elsewhere in the organization results in wasted effort.

Gate 3: Will anyone notice?

'OK, I can negotiate a tighter spec on the cap width and yes, I suppose that will make the line run more smoothly, but who is going to notice? Production will probably just say they are more in control of the process, besides plenty of other things will probably go wrong anyway.'

Purchasing is strongly dependent on other areas to be effective. Many purchasers have also been the unsung heroes of organizations and hold the belief that they are rarely thanked or noticed for what they do.

Gate 4: What's in it for me?

It is particularly easy to fall at this last gate. Often, the proposed benefit is too far removed from the individual. It is popular to encourage people with the thought of 'enhancing shareholder value'. But this is meaningless to most employees. Secondly, managers sometimes offer rewards they might like but which will not suit others. A night at the opera may not be everyone's idea of a good time.

Leadership styles that work best for purchasing

Of course a good leader is going to get results, with purchasing as well as any other group. The problem is that the business world appears to be short of good leaders, so most of us mortals need coaching.

The one thing all leadership models have in common is that they describe a spectrum of leadership styles, which broadly speaking have Adolf Hitler at one end and Mahatma Gandhi at the other. They use descriptors such as 'coercive' or 'coaching', 'democratic' or 'authoritative'. Many of them adopt the concept of 'situational leadership' as the best model; that is, have three or four styles you can adopt and use them appropriately depending on the individual or circumstance.

This is all good advice, and yet many of us struggle to master the one or two innate management styles we have, let alone nimbly stepping between a wide variety of styles.

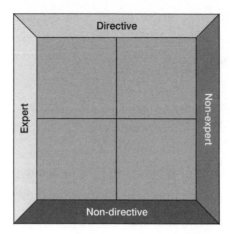

Figure 2.1

Rather than look at a spectrum, you could consider a management map or territory that you can walk around (see Figure 2.1).

In the top left corner, you are the expert and you are telling people what to do. This is great for situations where they don't know, especially when there is high risk. If you are teaching people the crucial knot to tie for a successful abseil attempt, the last thing you want is some sort of 'discover it for yourself' type instruction.

In the bottom left you know what to do, and you are working to coach the individual in their own way, perhaps with the occasional guiding hand. The risk of failure may be real, and it may be worth letting occur once in a while as part of the learning curve.

At the bottom right is true coaching. You don't need to know the answers because the employees almost certainly do, you just need to coach the right answers out of them. Risk can actually be quite high here, because the individuals know that you are not an expert and can make their own judgements.

The top right does not have a place in management. It may be fine for a lively pub quiz debate, but nowhere else.

In purchasing terms, the best place to be is probably middle left. The core nature of many purchasing people means that they will probably prefer some kind of guidance.

This is a challenge for new managers or, in bigger organizations, management protégés earning their spurs in purchasing. They may need to retreat at least initially to the bottom right corner, asking older hands for their input.

However, as soon as some of the concepts have been picked up, some elements of directive management will be valuable. The independent streak in most buyers will be strong enough to resist a completely daft idea, but without direction they are likely to stick to what they know best, and that may not produce any new ideas.

The danger is that managers spend too much time at the top left, expertly directing people based on their own purchasing experience. It can be quite destructive to keep setting the pace for independently minded people. Although it is rare to find managers who do this in an aggressive or bullying manner, far more widespread is the 'helpful' manager who pops by to see how you are getting on and makes suggestions. This is the same manager who says 'run it past me before that goes out'.

When you are an expert it is incredibly difficult to be non-directive. Even the most casual of comments can be excused as simple encouragement, yet can contain a direction: 'I really liked that savings graph on page 2, that is just what I think we need to be showing them.'

The principle therefore, if you do have a history in the discipline, is to work hard at being non-directive. It is a very different matter to say: 'The way you presented the data was spot-on. What made you think of putting it in that format?' Keeping this as a steady rudder setting will help counteract the strong winds of your own expertise, as well as the siren call of your employees for help and guidance.

Developing purchasing people

There has been recent recognition of the need for more development in purchasing, and some organizations are starting to put money behind the previously empty words to be found in their annual reports that people are their most valuable asset.

There is also a range of government initiatives to help smaller companies train staff. Two things need to happen to make development effective. First, managers need to put their staff and themselves into the queue for resources. This is not as easy as it may appear. Groups such as sales or engineering have usually had many years of established courses or links with universities. They may already be consuming decent chunks of training resource. The second issue is deciding what exactly you are going to train them in.

Training and development options

There is a difference between training skills and developing attitudes. In simple terms, skills can be considered 'what you do' and attitudes can be thought of as 'how you do it'. Historically, the emphasis has tended to be on skills training. In other areas there is a growing realization that you only get the biggest improvements when you tackle both (see Figure 2.2).

In the area of safety training, for example, it is likely that you will put employees on a course for 'lifting heavy objects'. However, real advances in safety only start to work when employees change their attitudes and develop an attitude that will lead them to avoid risks in the first place. The same is true for commercial skills and attitudes.

Some areas are clearly skills based. You need to understand how working capital affects the bottom line so that you can negotiate deals that reduce stock, for example. The basics of contract law or the rules governing tender placements can simply be learnt, as can the use of systems, the Internet and spreadsheets.

Figure 2.2

At the other end is development that will involve more subjective work. You cannot simply pick up a book on how to have personal impact and learn it. You will need to be more engaged with the process, practise it, get feedback and be coached.

Many key commercial skills fall between these two. People who have been on a basic presentation course can go through all the right actions and yet still produce a stilted and wooden performance.

Worse still, they could have attended a PowerPoint course, presenting you with lurid coloured slides in which great swathes of information flash, spin and pop up, all to the accompaniment of annoying hoots, whistles and the screeching of tyres.

Negotiation is a core craft of buyers and sellers and is a real combination of skill and attitude. You do need to know that a BATNA is not something you hit your supplier with but in fact your fallback position (Best Alternative To Negotiated Agreement). You need to know that when your supplier is talking about the Treaty of Rome this is not a freebie to Italy but an invocation of important anti-competitive legislation. These are simple facts that can be learned.

You also need to know how to get angry by design and not by default, how to stop bits of your body giving away the fact that you are nervous, and how to put your thoughts in order to achieve the desired effect.

These are the sorts of areas where learning about emotional intelligence, language patterns and your own limiting beliefs can make a real difference to your basic skills. These are empowering and enhancing developments. However, without really knowing how to use these skills you will simply be a golfer on the first tee who has read the rules of golf and bought a fancy set of clubs.

Strategic versus administrative

As part of helping purchasing people to develop, the move towards more strategic and less administrative work for buyers is increasingly being seen as the elixir of life, not surprisingly with the potential benefits it holds. A strategic approach:

- yields bigger savings;
- enhances job status;
- stimulates new thinking;
- saves on administration;
- makes the department sexier.

All of these can be realized if the transition is managed well. At the same time, the following can also happen if the people or processes are not robust enough to cope with the change. It can mean that:

- theoretical rather than practical strategies are produced;
- strategy is thought about but not deployed;
- administrative tasks are dropped and problems arise;
- employees become stressed;
- administration time is saved but there is no saving of manpower.

This transition is therefore high benefit and high risk. There really can be savings and attractive roles can be created, but equally you can end up with stress and stock-outs. The management skills needed to avoid the problems are simple enough, although some decisions could be tough and will require a good degree of honesty.

There needs to be a really clear definition of what 'strategic' means to your business. There must at least be some idea in your mind as to how a more high-level approach is going to yield savings. And you have to be sure that your staff are capable. In many ways you are delegating a new task, so the simple delegation checklist is a good one to use:

- Do you have the authority to delegate this task?
- Do they have the skills?
- Do they have the resources?
- Do they have the time?
- Do they know what the outcome is meant to be?
- Is there a good reason for them to want to do it?

It may be easy to tempt new graduates into doing more strategic work and probably harder to keep them focused on their core day job. However, more experienced buyers may not want to do this. They already feel that they are doing a good job, probably believe that their career prospects are pretty levelled out and they don't fancy the jargon that senior management appear to spout about strategy, which they think is plain common sense.

In these circumstances, assess the situation from their perspective and work hard to find the reasons why they should want to do this. Likewise, plan the way it will be enforced, which could involve anything from a coercive appoach to coaching.

Concluding thoughts

Unless you have just plucked your entire department from a desert island, they will have some inherent characteristics. In general these will tend towards the more technical, achievement and independent end of business behaviour. Adopt a management style that takes this into account. Everyone needs motivation. Some get it from within, but most get it from external influences, which is where you have a role as a manager.

Situational management is the key to success, adapting your style to fit each occasion and person. However, many managers have yet to master their own inherent style of management, let alone switch between approaches as strategies or people dictate. There is a tendency to give expert advice when you are an expert yourself. The more this can be countered by a reflective and coaching style, the more you will develop your staff and create a climate of self-motivation.

Developing your people must be a key target. There is a good argument in favour of having some of your staff technically qualified, but this should not be an end in itself. Look to develop their interpersonal and communication skills. They need the tools and the rules, but these are worthless if they cannot be used effectively.

3
The Position of Purchasing

WHERE SHOULD PURCHASING BE PLACED IN AN ORGANIZATION? This is a question that many are asking. Nevertheless, it is a surprising one. Just think how different it sounds to say 'Where should manufacturing be placed in an organization?' or 'Where should sales be placed in an organization?' These statements sound somewhat daft: manufacturing is manufacturing, surely it is a group in its own right? Sales may perhaps go in with marketing, but it's so obviously a commercial function – it just is sales.

Purchasing is unique: the nature of its work means that it gets involved with both ends of the business process and quite a few bits in the middle too. It bridges the relationship between production and sales and yet could be heavily aligned to R&D. At the same time, much of its functional activity is integrated into distribution or accounts.

The reason that purchasing has got itself into this itinerant state is largely due to its mixed heritage and its emerging status as a power in its own right.

The roots of purchasing

Many purchasing groups have their roots in manufacturing. The UK has a wide range of service industries so these will be different, but the important concept here is 'roots'. There are plenty of modern, centralized purchasing functions occupying flash new office suites in business parks with not a fork-lift truck in sight. As you visit them you get the impression of a very independent group. On starting your warm-up conversation with the buyer, the truth is quickly revealed. You find that they moved here three years ago, amalgamating several buying groups that were dotted around the country based at the production plants.

If you visit a major company that has all its facilities on one site, you also get a glimpse of this heritage. You park up and wait at the main reception. As an experienced sales rep you initially assume that your long wait is all part of the buyers' softening-up process, torturing your mind by forcing you to thumb through backdated copies of their company magazine. Not so: the delay was simply caused by the time it took the buyer to get there. When you are eventually greeted you start your long journey down corridors, out the back, across the road, through the shed and into the purchasing department – somewhere near the plant.

Many purchasing groups have been working hard to escape this heritage and to establish purchasing as a commercial function in its own right. Even if this transition to independence is not successful, many organizational structures have evolved that moved purchasing into other areas, sales and marketing, or perhaps accounts and IT. Where purchasing fits best is a useful question to ask.

Alignment with production

The kind of business you are in and the market challenges you face will be strong determinants of how to structure your group. Figure 3.1 is a SWOT analysis – showing the strengths, weaknesses, opportunities and threats – of one option, alignment with production, noting the benefits from business groups that are organized that way.

For many groups the alignment with production or manufacturing will already be their natural position. Even in non-manufacturing service industries such as hospitals or airports, they may well be heavily aligned to operations. In these business types the operational groups are in effect the production units for the services that they provide.

Strengths	Opportunities
• Close to primary user – good communication • Stock control options – can reduce them • Production plan changes quickly known • Technical and specification knowledge is good	• Purchase options to improve efficiency • 'Fit-for-purpose' specification can reduce costs • 'Cost-cutting' options, by looking at process • Exploit completer/finisher skills
Weaknesses	Threats
• Lack of commercial skill base • Further from end customer • Purchasing only seen as expeditors • Short-term focus	• Specifications dominated by ease of production • Focus on price not cost • Supplier contact too intimate – secrets given away • Aggressive approach to supplier management

Figure 3.1 Alignment with production

The benefits of alignment with production are going to come from the strength of communication and understanding. As a buyer you may have proudly struck a deal that takes 20% off the cost of packaging. If you are easily called to the packing line by a work colleague to watch the new batch of plastic caps fall off every bottle they are fixed to, it is going to heighten your sense of ownership to make things work. Likewise, you are bound to have a presence on senior management committees, and the fact that you are at these meetings can make a difference.

Production is often criticized for keeping problems from the rest of the organization. It is caught on the horns of a real dilemma. By their nature most production lines are at any point about to have a major problem that will affect production drastically. Production is very resourceful at solving these issues. If it flagged every possible problem, the rest of the organization's functions would not only lose faith in it, they would probably ask it to communicate less and stop crying wolf all the time. If you are at regular production meetings, then simply picking up that the new product runs are going slower than expected ('but don't tell marketing yet because we may get it sorted') can help to manage suppliers and stock. You can make your own judgement on these issues, adding in your extra knowledge concerning how fragile your supply chain is.

There is likely to be a higher technical input to buying decisions when you are close to production. This is a two-edged sword. On the one hand, you can make more confident decisions in marginal situations. There will be scenarios where the delivered product quality is slightly off specification. You have some choices: you could turn the lorry away and risk a stock-out, or you could accept the product at a discounted price, balancing this against the effects that you know it could have in production. Quick and confident decisions are important.

The decisions can be even more effective if they have some joint element of responsibility. If you are on the production line, then calling out the shift manager to look at the slightly damaged product can be critical to making it work well: he or she will be informed about its risks and will certainly adjust production to help cope. If this is a decision that was taken 200 miles away at the end of the phone, it is the easiest thing in the world for production either to disown the issue, or worse still to try to cope and let it pass without offering feedback to get improved product quality.

The challenge of being close to production lies in getting caught up in only chasing production targets. You may know all the benefits that could come from a new supply source, but you are also very sensitive to all the risks. Production-driven environments can be overly conservative when it comes to taking this type of risky decision. If things are going relatively smoothly in production, your chances of getting a new supplier introduced are going to be slim.

If you are close to any group it is only natural that some of their culture will become your culture. For purchasing really to add value there needs to be a 'stretch dynamic' between purchasing and production, some sort of productive tension. This may occasionally end up looking like a blazing row where both parties prod one another's chests and shout a lot. It is also the way in which you find out how new things work.

Alignment with accounts and IT

This tends to be the model favoured by companies who are in the service sector, where several factors come together to make it a logical choice. In this sector there will be higher business-to-consumer (B2C) sales compared to manufacturing, where business-to-business (B2B) is more prevalent. This focus on the consumer can mean that the functions of sales and marketing tend to be very consumer-centric. Purchasing departments are by their very nature B2B, so there is no natural link with sales. There is not usually any 'production' function in existence to team up with either. Compared to many other industry types, the major purchases are often of IT and accounts services. This alignment is certainly not exclusive to service industries; there are also a wide variety of other company types who have chosen to place purchasing here.

The strength of this structure can be in tackling transactional efficiency, which is one of the more hidden challenges that many purchasing groups face. If you are not very efficient then often people are working really

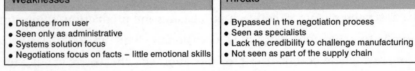

Strengths	Opportunities
• Seeing the financial impact on the bottom line • Transactional efficiency – e.g. invoices • Cost clarity in the chain • Numerical analysis skills	• Exploiting e-commerce • Fiscal options – tax savings • Systems integration • Administrative savings
Weaknesses	Threats
• Distance from user • Seen only as administrative • Systems solution focus • Negotiations focus on facts – little emotional skills	• Bypassed in the negotiation process • Seen as specialists • Lack the credibility to challenge manufacturing • Not seen as part of the supply chain

Figure 3.2 Alignment with accounts and IT

hard, running around just to keep things going – the department looks thriving and active. This in itself may not be good and it is a tough management issue. If you see three people in an office quietly reading, there is a natural tendency to think that they don't have enough to do and that the processes they are running are inefficient. Even if on closer inspection you found that two were reading a trade magazine and one was deep into a book on '*kanban* supply chain techniques', you would probably still have a management muscle twinge suggesting that they were somehow slacking and there was room to take out waste – yet their processes may be the most efficient.

The key benefit of improving this efficiency is, in reality, a lower headcount. There is also the chance to free people up from more mundane work and let them do more value-added activities. If numbers reduction is your target, then this organizational fit is the best one. If you are taking over a purchasing group that has all the accounts and IT-related activities in the same place, opening the office door on day one is bound to reveal a tempting target. Serried ranks of clerks and piles of invoice papers on the desk can be an easy stimulus to focus on this area as one way to save money.

If, however, this same activity is dispersed between several production plants, not only is it difficult to see, extracting the numbers is a challenge. Where there are small groups of transactional staff they often take on a variety of additional roles that make the specific transaction time you are looking to reduce hard to extract. You can do a careful calculation that delivered a 1.38 people headcount saving, and yet this is not deliverable in practice. Small groups can quickly fall below critical mass for shift and holiday cover and any staff turnover becomes a major management hassle.

An accounts and IT bias can have a real benefit if a move towards e-commerce is where you need to be. Systems solutions are both expensive and require a degree of technical knowledge. This technical skill extends beyond merely the IT specification. Systems rarely deliver on their full promise and a blend of technical and commercial skills is needed to encapsulate the delivery of service (or lack of it) into a contractual and commercial arrangement that is workable.

The management of fiscal and financial purchasing opportunities is also an area that can be more fruitfully explored if you are more closely linked to accounts. Most purchasing departments are aware of simple financial measures such as getting your working capital down at the year end or the need to push payment terms out. Closer liaison with accounts can reveal opportunities even in these areas. The buying of many utilities, rates and insurance is often overlooked by purchasing, but it is an area of concern to accounts. Likewise, accounts may know that a VAT rebate payment has just come in and this short-term cash richness means that you need not obtain an early payment discount from one of your suppliers. Working with accounts rather than using the function as an excuse for the directive that 'all payment terms have to be extended' can avoid the potential damage that such blunt approaches can have on supplier relations. If this area is to be used as a negotiating tool, precision targeting and open ownership of the commercial consequences will always achieve a better result.

This way of organizing does have its downsides. If you are dominated by IT, system-based solutions can often be seen as the key tool for success. Complicated sales and operations planning (S&OP) databases and excess automation can leave you over-informed to the point of ignorance. A system may be telling you that the truck has not arrived because it has not logged in yet, and thus trigger a chain of reorders or changed schedules. But a human being called Ron can actually look out of the window and see that there is a bit of a queue at the barrier and the delivery is certainly there, but will take an hour or two to be registered.

There is a danger that purchasing becomes seen as a process function, mainly focused on either transactions or dealing with data 'after the event'. It is always a challenge for buyers to become involved early enough in the buying cycle. If the members of your group are seen as system 'techies' or bean counters, you are not going to get the respect and involvement you need to have an impact. Accounts and IT are rarely given the credit they deserve within a business. If you associate purchasing with these functions, you may have to put in a little more effort to show your dynamism and attract the best talent from within the company.

Alignment with sales and marketing

This works well in situations where there is either only a small manufacturing or processing phase, or where the end product is regularly developed to meet consumer demand. Organizations like this are also the most likely to develop stand-alone purchasing functions, where the

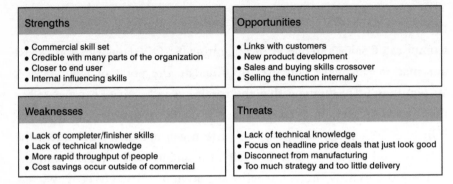

Strengths	Opportunities
• Commercial skill set • Credible with many parts of the organization • Closer to end user • Internal influencing skills	• Links with customers • New product development • Sales and buying skills crossover • Selling the function internally
Weaknesses	**Threats**
• Lack of completer/finisher skills • Lack of technical knowledge • More rapid throughput of people • Cost savings occur outside of commercial	• Lack of technical knowledge • Focus on headline price deals that just look good • Disconnect from manufacturing • Too much strategy and too little delivery

Figure 3.3 Alignment with sales and marketing

importance of purchasing is more visible in the overall company structure.

Once again, the benefits are simple. If you are in the personal care products market, then product development, package design and marketing launches are all critical to purchasing success. Working closely to form a bridge between marketing, R&D and your partner suppliers can make purchasing a real enabler in new product development.

It is of course possible to do this with other alignment models. However, if you all report to the same boss and are part of the same open-plan office, experience has shown that knowledge does 'leak' between groups, and this can make a difference. Links to customers (i.e. real external ones!) can also be made easier by this alignment. This not only helps see the end-to-end process, it also helps forge stronger relationships with key customers, which can be of genuine added value.

Modern purchasing requires a broadening in commercial skills. Sales and marketing have a greater tradition of investing in more holistic development of their people. Sharing in these development opportunities will certainly enhance buying skills. There is also a payback the other way: sales people will always benefit from seeing how professional purchasers are trained, and being part of the same group can help this happen.

As many production managers know, the commercial world can be quite airy-fairy. There is usually a range of hot-air initiatives, headline-grabbing savings claims and little follow-through. This is the challenge of being close to sales and marketing. If you lose the respect or contact with production, then maverick buying, inflexibility on specifications and high minimum stock requirements can easily come into play.

Commercial groups have a faster throughput of staff. More cynical folk believe this is so that they can avoid their poor decisions and empty promises catching up with them. Another view is that sales and marketing people do strive for the new, and would rather create something than complete it. Purchasing has suffered in the past from being a career backwater. Even today you are far more likely to find several really seasoned buyers in a group, yet you are unlikely to find brand managers of the same duration. In this set-up you will get more new faces in purchasing, and this will generate new ideas and fresh ways to tackle old problems.

Purchasing as a stand-alone function

This is probably where most major companies have moved, a purchasing group that sits in its own space. It is worth checking whether this has

Strengths	Opportunities
• Independent view • Seen as important/equal in company • Challenge all parts of the organization • Attractive to top talent	• Group-wide deals • Can make strategic relationships • Negotiation options using other departments • Critical mass to invest in skills
Weaknesses	Threats
• Seen as 'the police' • Central deals may have little roll-out • Often not linked to administration • Poor data control – head office not kept informed	• Alienation from other departments • Become too distant – a vocation not a role • Low staff turnover causing complacency • Poor line management for distant locations

Figure 3.4 Standing alone

fully occurred: there is still a real dearth of main-board purchasing directors. You find many companies who claim they have an independent supply chain organization, only to find that at the very top it in fact reports to the manufacturing director.

Car manufacturers were probably the leaders in this area. They recognized that with no integration into their own raw materials, the purchasing lever was a major one they could pull. As they developed into even bigger corporations the leverage became more powerful, uniformity of demand grew stronger, and competition meant that 'top-line' growth was not going to be an option. Car prices were coming down, not going up, so bottom-line savings had to be the centre of attention for increased profits. These pressures combined to form some of the first, and possibly most feared, of the independent purchasing groups. Many other industries are also facing those pressures.

The transition of the profit equation is an interesting one (Figure 3.5). All businesses will go through this equation at some time in their life cycle.

$$\frac{Costs + Profit}{= Price} \qquad \frac{Price - Costs}{= Profit} \qquad \frac{Price - Profits}{= Costs}$$

Figure 3.5

The speed of the transition is increasing, and what used to take several years back in the 1950s now can now be seen in several months. The first computer companies did not feel the pace of this change in the same way as mobile phone companies are feeling it now, for instance.

As the equation develops, so the criticality of costs increases and hence the pressure to boost the importance of purchasing so that it becomes a group in its own right. In the first sum, you simply add your margin onto the costs and you have your price. Some of the more expensive consultancies still operate in this way, so getting costs down is not so critical. The second equation is usually a painful transition phase, where many companies started to feel price competition and had not addressed costs sufficiently to stay in profit. Many manufacturing companies in the 1990s suffered from this and have now been consolidated as a consequence. The last of the calculations has the price subject to competition and the profit subject to shareholder demands – there has to be a return. On this basis costs are all critical, as some of the new budget airlines are now demonstrating: they have to focus on this lowest line with all their attention.

When these are the pressures a business is facing, a stand-alone purchasing group is more likely to be able to take the independent and challenging decisions that are needed to hit costs hard. It may well have the critical mass not only to attract top talent, but also to offer a career path in order to increase 'dwell time', the time people stay with the company. This forms a virtuous circle of professional development of individuals and that investment in training being repaid.

The downsides of this structure come mainly from the transition that can occur when independence turns more into isolation, or perhaps even arrogance. Purchasing needs to be strong and challenging, *and* it has to have the support and trust of all those with whom it works. Group deals, focusing spend on key suppliers, quality feedback from users and lack of maverick spending are all factors that rely heavily on relationships. Provided that the stand-alone group can stay engaged with its core internal customers, it will thrive on the benefits of independence.

Forming an independent group is not a game to be played at. Critical mass is important, there needs to be senior-level support, and purchasing needs to be genuinely of value to the company. The process of drawing together your purchasing group brings with it the full range of normal organizational restructuring challenges, plus, given the integrated nature of purchasing into many areas, a few extra ones just for purchasing.

Purchasing positioned as a profession

There is a growing body of opinion within purchasing that it should be positioned not only as a more professional group, but actually as a profession in its own right. The concept is that a combination of exams, experience and excellence could move the role of buyer to one akin to a lawyer or an accountant. Organizations such as CIPS have put a set of training and qualification processes in place that are both comprehensive and accessible to students and business people alike. You find a growing number of job advertisements saying 'CIPS qualification would be an advantage' and it is increasingly being seen as a credible commercial qualification. This idea has great merit in terms of increasing the skill of the buying role; however, professions carry with them disadvantages that will not help purchasing get itself into the right position.

A profession, as opposed to a department, occupies a unique position within an organization. An example that many people have experienced is the position of consultants in the structure of a hospital. They may well be employees of the NHS trust and there is a chief executive of that organization, yet despite this they hold an independence that is often hard to challenge.

Within the business world the same is true of legal departments. They are usually a centralized function and positioned close to the board, which in theory would place them very much 'inside' the organization, yet they are not. 'You had better run that past legal to see if we can do it' is a common phrase for most senior managers. Lawyers who are several management layers below the decision makers can overturn plans and cause things to be done in a different way.

To a lesser extent this happens with accountants. For example, sometimes accountants will be asked to structure business deals in an inventive way that keeps the outcome on the right side of the balance between tax avoidance and tax evasion. Once again, however, there will come a point when whatever the business strategy and aspirations to make certain claims, the professional rules of accountancy will intervene and the business will have to change its ideas to follow the rules.

It is possible for purchasing to move down the path to becoming more of a profession. If more jobs require CIPS qualifications then, increasingly, the profession will become more introverted. Part of the logic is to allow more careers to be created in purchasing roles. Although this may be true, at the same time it may start to isolate purchasing from other commercial functions. It is very rare to find accountants who take a career move into sales or marketing, for example. While it is always fun to insult the accountancy profession, some of them would make very good commercial managers and it would certainly be refreshing to find a marketing manager who could calculate their effect on the bottom line. Nevertheless, accountants are fully down the professional route and it would be a shame if purchasing ended up in the same position. Even if purchasing needs to be stand-alone, it should be so in an inclusive manner, it needs interaction and movement between it and other commercial functions, and it needs to be positioned as an enabler, not as an enforcer.

This is not, however, an attack on becoming more professional. That would be both a worthy goal and, in some less-developed commercial departments, a very necessary one. To say that purchasing must position itself as more professional, but not as a profession, is not mere semantics. These are different positions within an organization and the latter will not help purchasing get to where it needs to be.

Concluding thoughts

In a world of enlightened managers with perfect communication skills, a common business goal and a strong sense of teamwork, it doesn't matter where purchasing is located or even what its scope of work is seen to be. Since these criteria appear to be in short supply, the way purchasing is positioned will affect its degree of control and integration.

Exactly where purchasing should be is always going to be a subjective judgement based on the type of company activity. The biggest shortfall in this area is simply that nobody has taken the time to work out where it should sit and what it should do.

Lastly, the fact that purchasing should control all purchases does not mean that it should necessarily be an independent group. In the rush to get purchasing recognized and gain that elusive seat on the board, there is a tendency to want to make it a stand-alone department. This may be appropriate, but it may not be, and unless the group is mature enough to stand alone it could end up being isolated instead of integrated.

4
Managing Your Customers

A S WE HAVE SEEN IN PREVIOUS CHAPTERS, THERE ARE MANY ways in which the purchasing department can operate. Consider the following two diametrically opposed scenarios.

The nightmare scenario

Most people avoid the purchasing department if at all possible because it always imposes its own solutions whether you like it or not, and those solutions never seem to work very well. Often purchasers insist on using suppliers that everyone knows are not the best available. People have had long-standing relationships with suppliers soured by the purchasing department insisting they are not the cheapest on the market, even though they are better in many other ways, such as providing good service and keeping you informed of any developments in their product range.

People from purchasing don't seem to know much about the various products on the market, the different suppliers and even the company's own activities. They don't have much experience – most have been drafted in from other departments for various reasons – and have no qualifications in purchasing or supply management.

The purchasing department seems to spend most of its time dealing with paperwork and doesn't get involved in discussions about what the organization as a whole is doing or where it is going. The head of the department is not very senior and doesn't seem to communicate much with higher management.

If you have a problem with a supplier, there's no point in talking to purchasing about it because they won't listen. They have their own ideas about how things should be done and they can't be budged. And there's no point in trying to get to know them so that you can discuss things more informally, because they don't mix socially with others in the company.

The best-case scenario

The purchasing director is an experienced and qualified professional who is liked and respected by colleagues at senior management level. They can see that the director produces results for the company. The purchasing department's members are on excellent terms with other staff throughout the organization. Relationships are relaxed but businesslike. People feel that they can be honest with the purchasing department about what they do and don't want. They can see that the purchasing staff know what they're doing.

The company's purchasing professionals are happy to work with their counterparts in other departments exchanging ideas and information. Those who use their services consider them helpful.

These services cover a range of skills and knowledge. The purchasers know how to research the supplier market in any area from office supplies to IT to consultancy. They know how to select the right suppliers and help their colleagues choose between them.

They are happy to take charge of any purchasing activities in the company. However, they are not prima donnas. They are willing to let colleagues in other departments take part in the process and even hand it over to them if they know what they are doing, although they like to be informed of any purchasing activities that are going on.

The purchasing department keeps good records and can be relied on to come up with accurate figures if asked.

Purchasers are considered an integral part of the company's operations, so they are involved very early in the research and development cycle. Everyone realizes that not to involve them would be a big mistake, because they have all sorts of useful ideas and knowledge to feed into the process.

Everyone feels relaxed about dealing with the purchasing department because its staff are pleasant and friendly and, above all, helpful. If anyone needs to find out how to get a good deal, discover a new supplier or draw up a contract, they know where to go.

You are a supplier too

Being a purchaser has its benefits. You have a stream of prospective suppliers turning up on your doorstep eager to please you and persuade you to buy their goods. They need the business and you will decide whether they will get it or not.

It's a powerful position to be in. In the course of their daily activities, purchasers typically survey what is available on the market and decide which suppliers will be given contracts. The purchaser is the customer, and the customer is king.

In reality, though, no one is in the unique position of being only a purchaser at all times. In the bigger picture, you are a supplier too. You have your own customers: the people in your organization to whom you offer your skills as a professional purchaser. How well you provide them with what they want will ultimately decide whether you – as an individual or a purchasing department – stay in business.

As a purchasing professional you are – or should be – a source of useful information to your customers. You should be able to advise on efficient ways of buying goods and services, producing contracts and organizing suppliers. You should be able to provide the information that people need to make sense of what is happening in the business. You are someone with whom your internal customers should be eager to do business.

The internal supply chain

Supply chains are normally thought of as being made up of organizations linked together, but it's useful to think of yourself as part of an internal supply chain within your organization (see Figure 4.1). You have your customers, who have their own customers, who have their own customers and so on. You may be answerable to an immediate line manager who is in turn answerable to the head of department. The department head is probably answerable to a senior manager who is in turn answerable to the managing director. The managing director is answerable to the management board and they must answer to the shareholders.

It's the same for anyone in any function. But purchasing professionals are at an advantage over the others because they understand how supply chains work better than anyone else. You can make use of your insights into the business of managing partners for your own benefit.

It's up to you to keep your internal customers satisfied for the good of the business that pays your salary and for your colleagues, but also for the sake of your own professional pride and because, like everyone else, you want to be liked and respected.

Ultimately, you need to keep your customers satisfied because your internal customers, like the suppliers for whom you are a potential customer, have a choice. It's very likely that they can, sooner or later, decide not to take advantage of the services you have to offer. And if too

Figure 4.1 The internal supply chain

many people take that decision, you will find you are ignored. In the end you will have nothing to do.

Conversely, if you succeed in pleasing your internal customers, your individual stock will rise and your department will gain in status. Everybody will win.

Winning business

Like it or not, you need your internal customers and it's up to you to find ways of winning them and keeping them.

The communications officer at a major international travel firm once related how she saw her purchasing department as nothing short of a nuisance who simply got in the way and made life difficult. Her job involved commissioning freelance writers to produce brochures and other written materials. Like anyone in this kind of role, she had a trusted team of professionals at hand, each with their own strengths and weaknesses and particular areas of interest, whom she would commission from time to time as appropriate.

The purchasing department saw things differently. They insisted that she must carry out the kind of formal process well known to purchasing professionals, including producing a written specification for the work to be done and holding a tendering process with at least three suppliers bidding.

In theory, of course, that approach is perfectly correct. Going through a tendering process is the only way to make sure you are getting value for money.

In reality, though, commissioning highly specialized work in a very limited labour market does not lend itself to that kind of process. It's more appropriate to sourcing commodities than the services of creative writers.

The purchasing department had failed to sell itself to the commissioning editor. It had made no effort, it seems, to analyse the particular market involved and to assess the needs of its customer, the commissioning editor, who would run a mile rather than engage with the purchasing department again.

The purchasing department undoubtedly has a role to play in this kind of procurement, as in every other area. But the sad fact of this kind of all-too-common situation is that the purchasing professionals involved were apparently unaware of the need to engage with their customer and sell their expertise. They apparently thought that all they needed to do was spell out the rules and expect everyone to follow them.

Know your market

The best purchasing professionals – like their counterparts in other functions – see it as part of their expertise to study the activities of their customers and work out how they can help. They see people in other parts of their organization as customers whom they need to keep happy, so they need to study their activities too.

In the case of the commissioning editor at the international travel firm, the purchasing department had failed to understand the needs of its customers. Like an old-fashioned state-run monopoly, it saw itself as having a right to exist and to lay down the law for the people it dealt with. In today's world people are more sophisticated and organizations are more flexible. Nothing is taken for granted any more, so you need to prove your worth.

The prerequisite for doing this effectively is to know your market. The people you deal with will have their own prejudices and their own ways of doing things. They may be totally the wrong ways from a professional purchasing point of view, but that is what they are used to and they may not take at all kindly to someone telling them to do things differently.

So, just like your own suppliers, you need to find ways of getting to know your customers and identifying how you can get them to take what you have to offer. You need to know what they do, what their values are and, just as important, what they are like as people.

How do you see yourself?

It may be worthwhile reflecting for a moment on how you see yourself in your organization. Discuss with your purchasing and supply management colleagues what you think your role is. Then ask what makes you think this. Is it simply that your image of yourself is the one with which you feel most comfortable? Or are you aware of pressures within your organization that squeeze you into a particular mould? What is your evidence for the image you have of yourself?

Even more interesting may be how others see you, and whether this matches your self-image. This is not just a question of touchy-feely analysis of the navel-gazing kind. It makes a difference to how you can operate.

If people see you as ruthlessly efficient and aggressive in your approach, they may not be prepared to approach you about something they suspect they may not be doing very well. On the other hand, if they are desperate to improve results, they may not be attracted to someone who comes across as thoughtful and slow to act.

Before you can create effective links with others in your organization you need to be clear about how you see your role as a function. This needs some radical thinking: what are you there for?

Many purchasing departments have never effectively asked themselves this question. The department has always existed and it's obvious what its role is. Nevertheless, in reality it's not always obvious. 'We've always done things like this' is a deadly phrase to hear in any line of business. The question it begs in return is: 'Why?'

In Chapter 3 we discussed how purchasing can be positioned in relation to the broader organization. Here, let's imagine various scenarios describing possible modes of operation for the purchasing department itself.

The administrators

Every business function involves administration as well as sexier, strategic activities. And just like secretarial or reception desk work, it should not be considered unimportant. Making sure that transactions are carried out efficiently and that good records are kept is just as important in purchasing as anywhere else.

However, it would suggest something were amiss if a purchasing department's main role were seen as being administrative – or purely strategic, for that matter.

The IT manager of a major energy company, eager to gain publicity for her own purchasing achievements, once brushed off an inquiry about her organization's purchasing department, saying it wasn't responsible for buying strategy. It only did the administration, she said.

This is a nonsensical way to organize the company. IT managers should concentrate on what they know best: making decisions about the company's IT needs. Purchasers should be given the chance to do what they are best at: striking a good deal. At the same time, of course, they should not get so carried away by thinking of themselves as strategic that they forget about the importance of good administration.

The police force

Rather like the situation at the international travel firm described above, some purchasing departments believe they are there to lay down the law and make sure everyone follows it. They believe they know best and should control every aspect of spending. Relatively little discussion is needed, as the purchasing department has negotiated some very good deals and it's up to everyone else to make sure they take advantage of them. Anyone who decides to do their own thing instead should be hauled up and reprimanded.

The trouble with this approach is that it takes no account of human nature. People like to be consulted. They like to think they are being listened to. They don't want to be told what to do, no questions asked.

This is particularly true in modern organizations where creative thinking is valued. A mindset that says 'I will do whatever I am told to' is not one that is likely to come up with interesting, innovative ideas.

The consultancy

Purchasing professionals who have trained in their field, gained qualifications and gathered experience in the wider world are very likely to have much to offer their colleagues in other departments. They know the supplier market. They know where to go for information on new markets. They know how to develop the best relationships with suppliers, and they have expertise in the tricky area of contracts.

In an organization in which purchasing is seen as an activity to be carried out not just by a centralized team but by people in all functions, this model can be the most appropriate. It means that purchasing professionals are there to offer training in how to get the best possible deals, not necessarily to negotiate the deals themselves.

This model of how a purchasing operation should be run is based on an understanding of what skills are involved and how easy it is for non-purchasing professionals to pick some of them up.

If you as a trained and experienced purchaser believe that you and your immediate colleagues are the only ones capable of carrying out effective purchasing, this model will clearly not suit you. Nor will it if you regard the purchasing department as a specialist operation that should not open its doors to amateurs.

Nevertheless, the decentralized model has its proponents. Purchasing veteran Richard Russell, for example, has developed a model that he calls Centre-led Action Networks or CLAN, which has been taken up by several companies. In essence, CLAN is based on the idea that professional purchasers are there to help others do better purchasing, not to take charge of it all themselves.

It probably works best in organizations that are spread out over large areas, as many international companies are nowadays. It would be impractical for a single centralized purchasing department to carry out all the procurement on behalf of employees in many countries in different parts of the world. It may be equally impractical for the company's offices in each country – some perhaps quite small – to have their own purchasing departments.

So the middle way may work best, in which purchasing professionals in a central department communicate regularly with those people in the company who do some purchasing, to make sure that they have the knowledge and tools they need.

Some purchasing departments have developed a more important role. They believe that they have a huge amount of knowledge that can be beneficial to others, but they realize that they must tread carefully if they are not to appear overbearing. Better to be invited in by a colleague who thinks you may be of some use in producing better results than to barge in shouting orders.

In most organizations this is probably the best line to follow. The question is how to make sure that people know what you have to offer and take advantage of it.

At the IT services company Unisys, the purchasing department decided to tell its colleagues what it had to offer as part of a major reorganization. The purchasers linked with communications staff to produce a series of posters proclaiming the benefits of using the purchasing department. 'When you need clever ideas to increase margin, communicate with procurement,' said one poster. 'Team up with procurement and find a business partner fast,' said another.

The idea is simple: if people don't seem to know what you do, tell them. Let them know what kind of activities you can help them with. Then, if they can see that you have something to offer, they will come knocking on your door.

Be effective

None of the above ways of working is right or wrong: all have their place, and a purchasing department can be any of them at different times.

The point is to be clear about what the role is and to be effective in it. If there is a need for some enforcement of basic rules on how to go about making purchases, the policing role may be called for. But if purchasing people are to act as a police force, they should find a way of doing so that will work. That probably means not simply laying down the law and expecting everyone to obey – a more persuasive means will be required.

In the same way, being able to act as a kind of internal consultant is important too, but will only work if the purchasing professionals are able to deliver the goods.

It's all about results

The time when institutions, companies, departments or individuals were accorded status and respect for who or what they were has passed. Nowadays it's all about results.

Purchasing departments need to be able to show that they can indeed achieve results for their customers, whether this takes the form of achieving lower-cost deals, sourcing better suppliers or providing more choice. You can't expect anyone to return to you just because of who you are. You need to make it worth their while.

So it may be a useful exercise to analyse precisely what you have achieved for other departments. You can, of course, do this yourself by reviewing all your dealings with other departments and working out what difference you have made to them.

However, perhaps the most effective way to find out what others think of you is to ask them. This can be an informal, person-to-person approach in the staff restaurant, at a company social event or casually at the coffee machine or water cooler.

Remember that perception is crucial: whatever you think you have achieved, it's what your *customers* think you have achieved that really counts. No end of charts and figures showing how much you have saved your customers will make up for a generally poor relationship.

More objectively, formal interviews or a questionnaire may be useful. These need not be complicated or time-consuming. The main objective is to gather quantifiable information that you can analyse and compare over time or between different functions.

Dealing with more than one customer

So far we have conceived of a situation in which you have one customer within your organization. The reality, however, is that you will probably have several. And just to make life more interesting, they will probably have different objectives for you.

Your finance department is very likely to be concerned about how much money you are saving the company. Your sales department will be interested in whether what you are able to source from suppliers will help them sell more. Your public relations department will want to make sure that you are not setting any traps by sourcing from unethical suppliers.

Like any professional, your job is to balance the demands of all your customers. It may not be easy, however, and this is where your skills as a negotiator will come in handy.

Ultimately your loyalty is to the organization as a whole and it may be that you need to discuss its mission statement or objectives – if it has them – to reconcile different points of view.

All this can be made simpler if links between purchasing and other departments are formalized to some extent. Forming cross-functional teams to manage projects is an increasingly common way of working, with obvious benefits. As well as enabling different partners to exchange ideas and information, it can help iron out any potential conflicts arising from apparently divergent interests.

Sell yourself

Good public relations management is essential for all organizations. No one can afford to do their best and hope everyone else will notice and be impressed. Companies and public bodies increasingly realize that they have to shout from the rooftops about what they are doing. They have to be prepared to answer questions about their activities, especially if things go wrong.

The same thinking applies, in varying degrees, to individuals and groups such as company departments. It is especially important for purchasing departments because of the low profile they often project.

Some purchasing departments are taking action to remedy this situation. One major telecommunications company went as far as to appoint a full-time public relations officer for its purchasing department, responsible mainly for dealing with its internal customers.

Purchasing needs to find its rightful place in the business hierarchy. The first thing you need to do is strut your stuff, show your wares and make others want your services. Find out what you are good at and market yourself: how you affect the wider community, what are the practical things you can do for them, how you can make their life better.

Next you need an influence plan, which should list named individuals representing no more than 10% of the company. If you need some help in formatting this you could ask your own marketing department.

Take your 10% target and use your carefully crafted marketing material with laser-like accuracy. Get up close and personal with the people you are aiming at. If you make it important, they will too.

Objectives

It's not only important to achieve immediate results for your colleagues in other departments who can make use of your expertise, but also to make sure that your objectives as a purchasing and supply management professional are in line with those of the organization for which you are working.

If your company is new on the scene and eager to build up a supplier base, you need to act accordingly by making sure that approaches from prospective suppliers are dealt with sympathetically. If, on the other hand, the message from top management is that you need to reduce the supplier base, you would do well to set your standards high.

A leading consultant tells how he once visited a major retail chain. The procurement director was downcast. 'All my hard work over the last three years building up good, long-term relationships with our suppliers has been for nothing,' he said. 'I've just had a memo from the MD saying I must immediately cut all costs by 10%.'

It was a blow to the procurement director's strategy. But the plain fact was that he had failed to operate within the objectives of the company, which was experiencing severe problems staying afloat. This was not the time to build long-term relationships but to cut costs.

The boundaries of purchasing

Which purchases fall within or outside the purchasing department's control is a constant challenge. For definition purposes, it is useful to differentiate between purchases that are 'out of scope', and those that are often described as 'maverick'. Many purchasing groups will find that some senior consultancy, legal or financial purchases may not be 'in scope' – they may well be considered the domain of the Board. This spending is therefore out of scope.

Maverick spending is where purchasing does have control of the area of spend – perhaps copy printing – and yet some departments continue to spend in this area outside of agreed contracts and with non-approved suppliers.

The scope of most purchasing groups is usually defined more by luck and history than design and strategy. The simple rule is that the money flowing out of the company (purchases) should be within the scope of the department. The only allowable exception to this would be salaries, although even in this area there is some argument for using buying skills to enhance options.

The traditional culprits

Each company will have its own anomalies regarding what is in or out of buying's control, often dependent on the size of purchase. For some consumer goods companies the purchase of engineering materials could easily be left to engineers. In contrast, an engineering company may have professionals buying its spares, but advertising purchasing could be left to a commercial manager.

These sorts of anomalies are perhaps understandable, if not acceptable. There are three other categories of out-of-scope buying that are both inexcusable and unacceptable:

- *Too ignorant.* Some areas are just not thought of as purchases. Rates, insurance, audit fees, facilities management and sometimes one-off capital purchases can be in this category.

- *Too sexy*. These are areas that non-buying individuals want to keep for themselves. Strategic consultancy, PR, advertising and buying in temporary staff can be in this area.
- *Too diverse*. This is where buying is often in small unit quantities and people don't see the bigger picture. Travel, office spares and IT equipment can often be bought by every person in the company.

Widening the scope

The target is to get hold of all purchases in the company, balancing that against the need to remain in cooperation with all other departments. If the scope is widened through mutual interest, benefits will flow; if it's more a purchasing 'takeover', you can be in for many years of guerrilla warfare on maverick spending.

As purchasing widens its scope of influence it is rare to find it greeted like the Seventh Cavalry coming over the hill. At one end of the scale it could spell the end of an arrangement that meant some pleasant days out at the races. Even at the more mundane end (paying local council rates, for example), when you buy something you feel you have some control. You definitely have some power and giving that up is never easy.

Realizing how people respond is probably the key to success. As influence is expanded, mistakes are likely to be made. You don't have the relationships, you don't know the history and it is a new product or service for you to buy. Just as you are trying to show what a good idea it was to take over that area of buying, things will go wrong. Someone will process an order for 100 units to be delivered, not realizing that the product comes in 10s, so you now have a 'strategic' stock for the next three years.

There are some simple guidelines that can help with the process of widening purchasing's scope:

- Start by acting as a consultant to other departments' purchasing. They can still do it, but you will help with advice.
- Consider taking over the administration. This may not sound very appealing, but it does actually give them something of value and increases your understanding of the purchase.
- Invite them to purchasing meetings – especially any that consider strategy. This helps them see that purchasing is a more specialist activity.
- Be careful in approaching suppliers. The last thing they want is a professional buyer getting into the process. If you can establish contact at a higher level than their contact, this can bring effective lobbying pressure.
- Organizational change occurs with depressing regularity these days, but it does provide the perfect opportunity to move boundaries. If you are already doing the administrative work then this can appear as a logical place to consolidate the activity.

Concluding thoughts

Purchasers are customers who often occupy a powerful position in relation to suppliers. But purchasers are suppliers too, like everyone else.

Your role depends on who you are dealing with. Your internal customers are those in your organization on whose behalf you are buying or those whom you are helping with purchasing.

'Keep the customer satisfied' applies to your internal customers as much as anyone else. This is important for the organization that employs you and for those you serve as internal customers. It's also important for your professional pride.

To make sure of being able to work effectively with your internal customers, you need to consider what kind of role will work best. The hardest thing is to imagine how others see you, but it's important to get this right.

There are many different kinds of role you can play towards your internal customers – and they are interchangeable. You can behave in one way towards one customer and in a completely different way to another. You can adopt different roles at different times to the same colleague. It just depends on what gets results.

Purchasing is often under-recognized, so it may be necessary to publicize what it can do. There are many ways of doing this, ranging from personal contact to full-scale publicity campaigns. Crucially, people need to know that you can help them and show real benefits.

5
Relating to suppliers

PURCHASING AND SUPPLY MANAGEMENT IS ALL ABOUT PERSONAL relationships. Facts and figures are important too: they can give you the measurements you need to juggle with prices, costs, volumes, delivery times and so on. But it's people who really make a difference and the relationships between them that create real value.

The market, technology and the business environment are like a sports stadium. It may have the most magnificent facilities, but only the players, with their unique strengths and motivations, can win the game when they get out there and play.

This applies to every branch of business but particularly to purchasing and supply management, which is all about knowing who to talk to, getting what you want from them and striking deals. Organizations, after all, are not things but groups of people. Organizations don't deal with each other, people do.

Apart from the purchaser's internal customers, the main people they deal with are those with whom they negotiate and do deals: their suppliers. So being able to relate to suppliers effectively is central to the skill set required by excellent purchasing and supply management professionals.

The options

How should purchasers relate to suppliers? This will largely be determined by how they think of the relationship. The way you behave towards people depends on how you see them in relationship to yourself – your close family members, friends and professional colleagues, for example, will all receive different treatment from you because of who they are. Just as with any other people in your life, with suppliers it's a question of how you see them and, following from this, what kind of role you decide to adopt in relation to them.

Suppliers will have their own view of the purchaser sitting across the table. But as a purchaser, you are to a large extent in the driving seat. You can mould the relationship in the way that suits you best. Sellers, by the nature of the market relationship, tend to defer to buyers.

There are as many kinds of relationship as there are people, but here are some broad approaches to how you might view your supplier.

Your enemy

Your suppliers are out to get you if you don't get them first. The suppliers' job is to persuade you by any means available to take their product and charge you as much as possible for it. So you must counter-attack by beating them into submission.

You are the commander of the allied forces and your opponent is the bad guy. Just like in a real war, the winning side – your side – is righteous. You will probably succeed in getting lower prices most of the time too, so that must be a good thing.

Treating your supplier like an enemy has the beauty of being simple. You know exactly where you stand and so does the supplier. Your objective is totally clear: to get the best possible deal for yourself, whatever it takes.

It may also make you feel good to go into battle with a definite result in mind. But the adversarial approach to purchaser–supplier relationships has a downside.

Suppliers come in all shapes and sizes. With some, an adversarial approach will work. With others, it won't. If your approach is consistently to beat your supplier into submission, you may be missing out on great deals that require a more subtle approach. But you'll never know.

There is always the risk, too, that the tables will turn. The purchaser may be in a strong position for the time being, but if the product being bought becomes scarce, the relationship will change.

For many years ICI supplied a simple calcium product. It looked like chalk and was valued about the same by the inks and sealants market who used it as a filler. But then scientists discovered that it had unique thickening qualities that enabled it to replace far more expensive polymers.

This meant that the price could go up 35% and it would still be good value. Concerned for some of its sealant companies with whom ICI had a good relationship, the increase was carefully phased. But there was one ink company that had always acted aggressively towards its suppliers, including ICI. Purchasers at that company were dealt the full 35% increase, all in one go. It was a simple case of take it or leave it. They had to take it.

Your servant

In this kind of relationship, it's as if your suppliers have been put on earth to satisfy your needs. It's their job to appear before you when ordered, displaying their latest offerings. You may pick and choose from these at your leisure, then dismiss the sales people to return to their humble abode.

You don't treat the supplier as an enemy because you don't need to. It's clear where the power lies – with you. This is what's known in legal jargon as a master–servant relationship. You dictate the terms on which you will do business and expect the supplier to kowtow. The purchaser is in an exalted position and expects the supplier to respect this.

The master–servant relationship is fine if you are the master, though not so great, of course, if you are the servant. It means that there is a huge imbalance of power: if your supplier is prepared to accept being treated as an inferior, it suggests that it desperately needs the contract.

The problem with treating suppliers as servants is that they are disempowered, and this is not in either side's interests. The supplier will not feel motivated to share information with the purchaser or to offer the benefits of innovation or improved production methods. There is little incentive when you have been forced into a subservient role.

Your partner

You are equals, working towards a common objective. You treat each other with respect. You are open and honest with each other, happy to swap information and ideas. You know that when your partner says that it can't lower the price any further, this is likely to be true. What's more, its staff will explain why they can't lower the price and show you the figures to prove it.

It seems like the perfect relationship. There's little point, after all, in wasting energy on subterfuge and clever negotiating tactics if you can avoid them and still get a good result. A partnership of equals reduces psychological wear and tear to the minimum because it's based on mutual respect. Everyone can get what they want and feel pleased with themselves.

Partnership is a fine thing, and there are many examples of this approach saving huge amounts of money, but partners confide in each other and this may not be advisable with your suppliers at all times. It may be better to keep your distance.

From the supplier's point of view, there is a big danger that 'partnership' is merely an excuse for the buyer to take an even more dominant role than in an openly adversarial relationship. Partnership is a two-way process, but suppliers have been known to complain that in reality it means purchasers delving into their books and production methods – with the risk of sensitive information becoming known to competitors – while the same freedom is unavailable in the other direction.

Your friend

A friend is someone for whom you want to do your best. You want them to be happy and to feel the same way towards you. You want your suppliers to like you because you need them and you hope they need you too. This is a personal relationship built on trust. It would be a big blow to your esteem if they were to let you down.

Be very careful with a relationship based on personal friendship. This is business, not dating. Get too close and you may regret it. And it may not look too good to your associates. On the other hand, if you're consciously using this approach to achieve a result, there may be something to be said for it. You are looking for a result and if forging a personal friendship helps with that objective, it may be worth trying.

Big problems can be caused when people confuse business and personal areas. It's good in business to be open, honest, engaging and friendly. But while the personal approach can coexist with the business relationship, they must not become codependent. The only time a purchaser should use the personal approach is to facilitate a business process, getting parties to start talking again, for example. Or, perhaps, when all other options have failed.

Flexibility

There is a natural tendency to go for simple, straightforward answers. There must be one way of dealing with suppliers that works best. One of the above approaches must surely be the right one. But the reality is that, as we have stressed, people are individuals. They need to be treated according to their personalities and circumstances.

All the above approaches may be desirable at different times but none is a panacea. It's up to the purchaser to decide what will work best at any given time. It means more thought and may be harder work, but a flexible approach is more likely to produce results.

All have advantages and disadvantages, depending on the circumstances. None of them is necessarily the best. They can all have their place in your toolbox as a professional purchaser.

Look at it from the sales person's point of view

It's easy to forget that it takes two to make a relationship. You have your own history, prejudices, beliefs, pressures and goals – and so does your supplier.

So, just as with a personal friend or partner, trying to see things from their point of view can work wonders. How does the purchaser–supplier relationship look from the other side of the table?

Sales people, like all serious professionals, work to a plan. They don't usually merely pick up the phone to you or turn up on your doorstep hoping for the best. They have clear objectives, just as you have yours. Usually these will be well-thought-out and incorporated into a marketing plan.

The purchaser needs to understand as clearly as possible what this plan may look like, because that will help you get a better deal.

Theories of buyer–supplier relationships

The way sales people deal with potential customers has been studied in depth and has spawned a huge literature. For a sales person, understanding how their opposite number thinks is crucial.

There is much less corresponding information available from the point of view of the purchaser, though that is changing as business realizes the importance of good purchasing. Nevertheless, some academics and business analysts have studied relationships between purchasers and suppliers. They are interested in finding out what kinds of relationships exist between those who are selling and those who are buying. They also want to know what works best from the purchaser's point of view.

If you think of a supply chain in the classic way as a series of organizations linked together, the relationship between buyer and supplier is clearly crucial at every stage. The weakest link in the chain can affect the whole operation – if goods or services are held up by one organization, or not produced to an acceptable standard, it will make the whole process less efficient.

Traditionally, relationships between buyers and suppliers often tend to be short term and based mainly on the question of price – the 'treating your supplier as an enemy' approach described above. But, as we have seen, this is not the only option.

In recent years the idea that supply chains should be based on much closer relationships became widely accepted as a better way to proceed. The partnership approach, or partnering, seemed almost to be official policy promoted by the government and other bodies.

Several government-backed reports have advocated partnering in the construction industry, for example, where a highly complex web of short-term, adversarial relationships is the norm in a typical building project. Construction traditionally suffers heavily from disputes between organizations, which often end up in court. According to the official reports, if companies were to work together in teams, exchanging information and cooperating, all this could be reduced to the benefit of all.

However, at the same time it has become widely accepted that different approaches suit different circumstances. As far back as the 1980s, a 'portfolio' approach was suggested as best practice. This is best portrayed

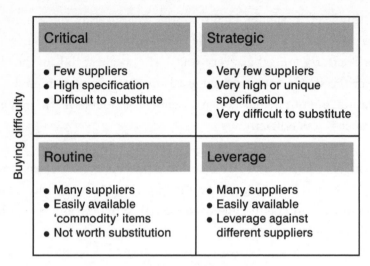

Value to the buying organization

Figure 5.1 Purchasing portfolio management
Adapted from Exhibit I in 'Purchasing Must Become Supply Management' by Peter Kraljic, September 1983, with permission of Harvard Business Review. Copyright 1983 by the Harvard Business School Publishing Corporation. All rights reserved.

by the purchasing portfolio management quadrant published by Peter Kraljic in 1983, showing four broad ways of dealing with suppliers. Figure 5.1 shows a similar quadrant based on Kraljic's model.

According to this analysis, purchasers should assess their suppliers according to two main factors: first, the value of the supplier to the purchasing organization; and second, in terms of the relative availability in the marketplace of the item or service supplied.

If an item or service is of high value but there are many suppliers who can provide it, it is best, according to this approach, to use 'leverage': the purchaser should use its market knowledge to push for the best deal possible.

If there are very few suppliers of an item or service of high value, the best approach is 'strategic': try to form a close, long-term partnership. 'Critical' and 'acquisition' approaches are in the same way based on an analysis of the supplier's value to the purchaser and the relative state of the supplier market.

This simple approach has been widely promoted as a basic tool for purchasers. In the meantime, though, it has been developed into far more complex analyses of how buyer–supplier relationships work. The main development has been to look at the relationship from the supplier's side as well as the purchaser's.

Professor Andrew Cox at the Centre for Business Strategy and Purchasing at Birmingham University has been a leading force in questioning the idea that partnership is necessarily best, and has also developed an increasingly more complex analysis of these relationships. He and his team argue that the relative balance of power between the two parties is the key to understanding what kind of relationship will work best. Partnership works well in some industries for some kinds of goods or services, Cox and his associates argue, but not for others. It depends on the circumstances.

In his latest book, Cox suggests that the relative scarcity and utility of the supplier's resources set against the same criteria for the purchaser will determine what kind of relationship is produced. So if a good or

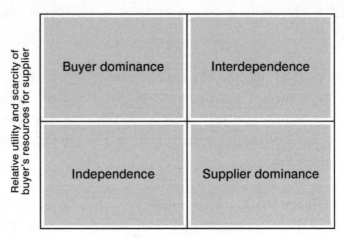

Figure 5.2 The power matrix
Reproduced from Andrew Cox, Chris Lonsdale, Joe Sanderson and Glyn Watson
(2004) *Business Relationships for Competitive Advantage*, London: Palgrave
Macmillan, with permission.

service is relatively high in value for the purchaser and also scarce, while
being low in value for the supplier and low in scarcity, the relationship
will be one in which the supplier is dominant. The other kinds of
relationship suggested by the analysis can be seen in Figure 5.2.

Put simply, the more strategic the item being purchased for both parties in
the deal – the more crucial it is to the objectives of the purchaser and the
supplier – the more a partnership relationship is likely to be effective.

Buying consultancy services, for example, or IT systems, or very expensive
pieces of machinery used in production is likely to be appropriate to long-
term relationships between purchaser and supplier based on collaboration

and mutual trust. But low-cost, low-importance items – office supplies, for example – can be bought from whichever supplier is offering the best price at the time. There is nothing to be gained from forging a close relationship with a small number of suppliers of notepads, pencils and paperclips. A better approach would be to try to aggregate as much spending as possible and push for the lowest possible price.

In one case study described by Cox, an aviation supplier in the South of England was having big problems with its supply chain. An analysis of where the hold-ups were occurring quickly revealed that one supplier in the chain was consistently failing to move the goods along to the next link in the chain. And the reason for this lack of urgency was immediately clear to the team from Birmingham: unlike most of the other organizations in the supply chain concerned, this was a major multinational that felt no particular need to prioritize a relatively very small amount of business while it had much bigger, more important contracts to fulfil.

This could be one of the few times when it is worth attempting to use friendship as a tactic: the supplier is not going to engage in a partnership and you have no leverage, so you may as well try to get as friendly as you can with your local contact and hope that it will work for you in their company. In the meantime, of course, it would be as well to look for another supplier.

Simply understanding why this is happening puts the supply management professional in a much better position to find a solution – perhaps by finding a more appropriate supplier or by renegotiating the contract with the existing organization. On the other hand, a purchaser or supplier assuming they are in a position of power over the other party, when in reality they are not, can create similar problems.

What it means in practice

In reality, relationships will appear to be of various kinds with no inherent logic to them. Some will appear 'tactical', more or less *ad hoc*, with no particularly close relationship between purchaser and supplier. Some will seem more 'strategic', where a longer-term view and a closer relationship are predominant. At the same time, the view of the relationship on either side may appear to be anything from adversarial – the 'treating the supplier as the enemy' approach – to one of trust, more in line with 'treating the supplier as a friend'.

This is not, however, merely an academic exercise. What follows is another, more detailed attempt to describe some of the main forms of relationship between purchasers and suppliers and what they imply in practice for particular kinds of activities (see Figure 5.3).

After all, it is of little use to a purchaser to know that a relationship with a supplier is tactical and adversarial unless it is also clear what that suggests in terms of action on such issues as benchmarking and demand planning.

Some purchaser–supplier relationships

- *Tactical adversarial.* In this scenario, the purchaser has the choice of many suppliers in the marketplace for a particular product or service.

The main focus in dealings with suppliers is on price, using volume leverage and regular changing of suppliers as tactics to maintain excellent deals. There is a very limited exchange of basic information, mainly by telephone or e-mail. Prices are regularly measured against those offered by other suppliers.

- *Tactical distant.* Several suppliers are available in the marketplace. Price is important but so is total cost, although service and quality are not extremely critical. Some information is exchanged, with the emphasis on the supplier doing the work. There are some visits by the purchaser to the supplier or vice versa.

- *Tactical involved.* There are relatively few suppliers available and the emphasis is on total cost and service more than price. Information about internal processes is shared. There is regular contact between personnel from either side. The purchaser may also look at second-tier suppliers. Benchmarking is carried out fairly regularly and there are some joint development targets.

- *Strategic committed.* Only one or two suppliers are available. There are likely to be longer-term framework agreements in place between purchaser and supplier. There will be regular and planned contact at several levels and clear visibility of information flow between organizations. Analysis of the supply chain and leverage are gained through cooperation.

- *Strategic trust.* In this relationship there is only a single supplier and the emphasis is on developing mutual benefits. There is likely to be detailed supply and value analysis. Information will be openly available on either side. There will be contacts between the organizations at the highest levels. Some assets will be integrated and there will be joint investment and development.

	Tactical adversarial	Tactical distant	Tactical involved	Strategic committed	Strategic trust
Supplier base	Many suppliers	Several suppliers	Supplier base is limited	Only a few big players	Single supplier
Benchmarking	Benchmarking is carried out on a reular basis	A significant amount of benchmarking	Some benchmarking – not just cost related	Limited benchmarking	Supplier led
Demand planning	Requisitions/ purchase orders	Blanket orders and call-offs	Regular sharing of schedules	Some joint systems for planning	Integrated supply plans
Negotiation style	Aggressive and changing	Powerful and practical	On tender, share some information	Work closely with supplier for mutual benefits	Open book costing
Wider business contact	No real activity	Occasional to solve specific issues	Some projects with wider contact	Regular teams meet cross-functionally	Shared work at both strategic and working levels
Open book costing	None	None	Share suppliers but not buyers	Yes for specific projects	Total
E-commerce	None	Reverse auctions	Auctions and automated standard processes	Some linked systems. Most paperwork automated and self-billing	Integrated systems

Figure 5.3 What different kinds of relationship mean in practice

Who should deal with suppliers?

Another key question for most organizations is to decide who should deal with suppliers. As we have already seen, in a well-developed organization the purchasing function is likely to be staffed by trained professionals who have the skills and market knowledge to secure the best possible value for money.

Nevertheless, it is not necessarily sensible to say that they alone should do all the purchasing. Too rigid an insistence that only the purchasing department should be responsible for buying is likely to lead to resentment, demoralization and a loss of efficiency.

At the same time, it is probably not ideal for the professionals to delegate all responsibility for day-to-day purchasing to people in other functions. That would amount to an abdication of their responsibility for making sure that purchasing is being done effectively and efficiently. The ideal situation is probably somewhere in the middle.

From bow tie to diamond

It's very easy to think of contacts between two organizations as being restricted to the key personnel: purchasers and sales people meeting from time to time to thrash out prices and other aspects of the relationship. But there are likely to be many other people in the purchasing organization who have an interest in the discussions. They should be encouraged to develop their own contacts with suppliers.

All of the layers of contact with suppliers should be developed. There will often be significant 'coal-face' contact, for deliveries, order placing and invoice administration. These are areas that sellers increasingly understand are valuable, and buyers should recognize this too.

For example, you can easily find out who else your supplier is dealing with and what kind of deal they are getting because drivers making deliveries talk to each other. This kind of market intelligence can be extremely useful. If purchasers talk to drivers, who talk to the supplier's drivers, there may be all sorts of benefits.

Think of it as in Figure 5.4 as moving from a 'bow tie' relationship, in which the point of contact is extremely narrow, to a 'diamond', in which there is the broadest possible relationship between the two organizations.

In this kind of situation the purchaser will want to maintain an 'enable and control' role. You don't want to control everything because it takes too much time and doesn't empower others, but at the same time you don't want to create an open house where your own sensitive information is likely to leak out.

The UK bank Abbey has made many advances in its relations with suppliers. One of its challenges was that the diamond had become too wide in some circumstances. Many IT contractors were fully integrated into Abbey's systems. This had great benefits in terms of mutual understanding and close relations. The challenge was that with contractors all holding badge passes and sitting in the same open-plan office along with permanent employees, it was going to be hard for suppliers not to see budget proposals, new potential projects and all the

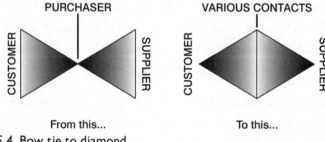

Figure 5.4 Bow tie to diamond

costing information they needed. This relationship had to be changed – Abbey didn't want to lose the intimacy with all suppliers, but total freedom to access data was not appropriate.

Leapfrog relations

Purchasers can also benefit hugely by relating to their professional colleagues in other organizations, especially those working for suppliers.

Members of the purchasing fraternity, like other communities of interest, speak a common language and have much to learn from each other. Engaging with your supplier's buying department could be a shortcut to potential savings and a better understanding of its challenges. There is nothing to lose from developing a relationship with your opposite number working for a supplier.

Senior-level contacts are also always worth developing with big suppliers. There are potential dangers – it may be nothing more than a talking shop – but the goodwill likely to be generated from such contact could be very useful to call on if negotiations run into trouble.

How to slice it

There are many ways to organize a purchasing function so that it is able to deal effectively with suppliers. All have their advantages and disadvantages.

It may make sense, especially for large organizations, to split purchasing geographically. Many companies divide their buying teams up in terms of Far East, Europe, Middle East and Africa (EMEA) and so on. There are advantages in developing understanding of other cultures and business customs. The downside is that this will encourage local patterns to emerge at the expense of consistency through all the regions in which you are operating.

Geographical regionalization can work well enough for the sales function, but buying often has a wider set of relations. Your factories may be in Europe, but you buy from all over the world. So it may not make sense to have buyers who specialize in dealing with companies in the Far East.

A common way to divide purchasing teams is by the kind of goods or services in which they are dealing. Designating 'categories' of spending is another way of creating specialization, which again has its advantages and corresponding disadvantages. The more a purchaser focuses on one particular category, the less they are likely to develop their knowledge of other goods and services.

The same consideration applies to the idea of dividing purchasers in terms of the size of purchases in which they are likely to be involved. The big question for management is to decide where the relative advantage lies.

The crucial point is that the way the purchasing department is organized should be by design, not by default. It can be very hard to step out of an inherited organizational model. Professional purchasers need, at some point, to go back to first principles and work out what kind of organization is appropriate to the given circumstances.

Going native

The drive in favour of partnership relationships has brought with it the new worry that if you fraternize with the enemy long enough, you might 'go native' and end up supporting its cause more than your own.

This is a bizarre turn of events. Buyers have always been seen as 'hard'. Indeed, the whole move towards a more partnering approach was driven by the idea that the adversarial nature of the buy–sell relationship was precluding significant benefits from being realized. To be accused of 'going soft on a supplier' is probably the most heinous crime a buyer can commit. Such sins are rarely talked about openly: there will be quiet words in high places and portfolios will be judiciously reshuffled.

Some say that buyers should be moved around on a regular basis to avoid this. Personnel changes within organizations occur naturally and turnover is in any case relatively high among the sales people with whom purchasers deal.

However, if partnering is properly carried out, with only a few, appropriate relationships, then going native is exactly what purchasers should do. The hope is that some of the other side will have done the same and this helps to redress any imbalance. Really understanding your suppliers, and seeing what value they can add to your business, is in fact the only way in which the tougher benefits are going to be uncovered.

A far more positive approach is only to consider moving your buyers away from an existing relationship when there is going to be a refreshing effect on your people. It is possible to develop a version of snow blindness when you have been dealing with the same supplier and products for a long time. A fresh pair of eyes can see how things have moved on, and previously tried solutions may now work. Likewise some buyers, while enjoying the strength that experience in a relationship can bring, may also benefit from new challenges in another area.

Concluding thoughts

Flexibility is the key to forging the most productive relationships with suppliers. Everyone is different and the expert purchaser needs a range of strategies. No single template holds all the answers.

The adversarial approach is one among many and has its uses, depending on circumstances. Partnership is also extremely valuable in some situations. Neither necessarily holds the key.

Relationships also change over time. A professional purchaser has a range of strategies and can use them as and when they are likely to be effective.

People are often good at spelling out how things should happen. They are often less good at putting the grand plan into effect. For purchasers, there is no point specifying what kind of relationship you have with a supplier unless it translates into action.

People relate to other people and purchasers should encourage contact between their colleagues and the suppliers with whom they deal. At the same time, purchasers should aim to keep such dealings under control.

6
Negotiation

NEGOTIATION IS A GRAND TOPIC THAT BRINGS WITH IT SOME worthy concepts: 'win–win', trust, partnership and contracts that forever change the way you do business. At the same time it has a dark side: lies and untruths, dirty tricks, broken trust and short-term thinking.

In real life a deal needs to be done. There are some simple skills to help individuals steer a course between the two extremes and end up with something of value. This chapter will look at the worthy concepts for what they are, lift the stone to shed some light on darker deeds, and give a practical framework to build successful negotiations.

Grand concepts

Trust in business

'How can I trust them?' This question is being asked more than ever because of the trend towards developing partnerships and longer-term solutions. It is all too often followed a year or so later by the other big question: 'Why did I trust them?'

The simple rule is that you cannot trust anyone in business. This is a lot less harsh than it sounds. It is not because people themselves cannot be trusted. Nor do you have to live by the conspiracy theory, that the rest of the universe is out to get you at the first opportunity. These kinds of views are not only wrong, but also lead to bad deals. They are self-defeating: if you hold them then at least one party to the deal is taking a defensive position, and that will never move the deal as far forward as it could go.

It is also not some kind of moral stance – the saying that there is always a 'sin' in business is not helpful either. Instead, it is built on the simple premise that we have lacked sufficient imagination to develop different words that reflect the reality of what goes on in business.

If you call things by different terms then it can have astounding effects on what people expect. For instance, many people in business bemoan the fact that forecasts are always wrong. They get the production or sales forecasts each month and they appear four weeks later to have been a masterwork of fiction. But a forecast is in fact a supposition, an assumed view of what will happen. In other words, it is a guess. People rely on forecasts. They would take a completely different attitude if you turned up to the production planning meeting and said: 'Here are the guesses at what we will need to do next week.'

The same is true of trust. It is a word that, if you can define it, is something that should be confined to personal relationships. We need a new term, 'business trust', which defines the different nature of the reliance that you can expect in a business relationship.

Trust is the belief that someone will continue to behave in a certain way even though you are not there, and that this behaviour will last over time. The problem in the business world is that people do not own their behaviour, it is rented. This is not an attack on corporate Big Brother; it is a way of looking at the reality. Everyone is an individual with their own feelings and desires. This individual could be described as the person at the heart of their activity, represented by the inner circle in Figure 6.1.

Outside of this is the behaviour they display. At work that behaviour is modified, because people are asked to behave in certain ways to meet their employer's needs. In return for this modified behaviour people are given money. Their behaviour is rented.

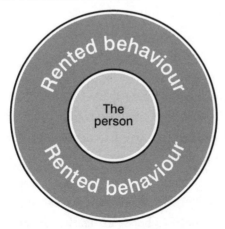

Figure 6.1

This explains why you cannot simply 'trust' people in business. They are not in control of their own behaviour, in which you are placing your faith. There was outrage when Dyson moved its production to Malaysia, and consternation when M&S switched its knitwear supplier offshore. 'We trusted them,' people cried.

In business these kinds of decisions need to be taken. You may have just concluded a deal a month ago with a firm price for a year and, barely with the ink dry, you are asking the other party back to talk about a further 5% reduction. This is where the concept of business trust is a more useful measure. It forces the parties to realize that although they may like each other, indeed may even trust each other personally and enjoy an open relationship, that is not the same as business trust.

Business trust is not to be based on the person, but on the other organization and the marketplace. The trust lies in the belief that the forces presently making this a good course of action will continue. You can only trust in continuing business metrics, not in the individuals who work within them.

Win–win

It is a shame that such a great concept as this has been so shabbily treated over many years. Just like its colleagues 'partnership' and 'trust', inappropriate and exaggerated use has demeaned these terms to almost meaningless catchphrases.

The underlying power of the idea is still a great one. If the deal that you strike is of genuine benefit to both parties then it will last, and it is likely to generate activity and information exchange that will broaden the benefits over time. Where it fails is usually because either party has not thought through two important areas.

The first point is to have properly come to terms with the real market you are in, and what sort of alternatives you have. In preparation for any negotiation knowing your BATNA is critical. You will remember from Chapter 2 that this acronym stands for Best Alternative To Negotiated Agreement – in other words if you cannot agree, what are you going to do?

Supermarket chains and some of the big car makers developed quite a reputation for 'win–lose' styles of negotiation. Many have worked on this and are changing their style, at least for some product ranges. Despite this, many suppliers to these chains have complained of being kicked around, with little regard for the benefits they were supposed to get from the deal. The problem was they did not appreciate their own BATNA. If they chose to set up their market offering to be heavily reliant on one or two major customers who control the marketplace, then frankly what did they expect? Likewise, if you are perhaps supplying white spirit to the paint industry, don't be surprised to be constantly at the auction table bidding on price all the time on a 'winner takes all' roulette game. The answer does not lie in hoping for some benevolent change to a win–win philosophy, it lies in getting the cost base right for your business to be able to deal in this marketplace.

The logistics industry has been particularly prone to this over recent years. There are many, many suppliers. While some are undoubtedly moving to offer higher added-value services that can support a win–win concept, many are still at the commodity end. Too much talk in that industry of partnerships, trust and benefit sharing has left many in the market disillusioned with the idea of win–win, perhaps because they find it hard to face up to the reality of their BATNAs.

The other win–win concept to consider is the personal one (see Figure 6.2). The Japanese have a well-developed sense of 'saving face', the idea being that you should always help your negotiating partner to look good even if the cards are not stacked evenly. In any negotiation there will always be some sort of win or loss – it is, after all, a process of trading one thing for another. The business person's dilemma is that there are going to be wins and losses at both a business and a personal level, and on both sides.

The more western style of negotiating does not pay enough attention to this aspect of personal win or loss, and at the same time it is overly

	Personal	Business
Win	Yours?	Theirs?
Lose	Theirs?	Yours?

Figure 6.2

reliant on personal trust. While you should not rely on personal trust in negotiation, an individual's personal stake in the outcome is worth considering and is often overlooked. This is not about pandering to their personal whims. It is all about the simple rule that if you make it easy for someone to accept something, they probably will.

This is important for buyers. Sales people often have less room for manoeuvre than buyers and more explaining to do within the organization. A sales person will rarely be the one to set pricing policy: they may only have interpretation within guidelines. A buyer, on the other hand, is often the sole arbiter of what the deal should be, especially if the price is reducing. In this scenario buyers should help sales people so that they can look credible when they go back to their product managers with a call that starts 'Well, the good news is that we got the volume we needed . . . '

Dirty tricks

Lying

Most sales people believe that buyers are liars. This will be by no means all the time, but at some stage in their career they will have had an experience that will make them believe this, and it is a very popular belief to hold. It does of course carry with it the equal and opposite force that most buyers believe that sales people lie at some stage too.

Lying in a negotiation is not a good idea. However, the way in which many people define lying can leave quite a wide scope of activity that can still apparently avoid the moral low ground of being called a lie, yet will easily mislead the innocent.

Two tactics to watch out for are using unconnected but true statements, and giving a positive answer to a different question than the one asked. Both of these also rely on a common fault, namely holding a pre-existing belief that is easy to take advantage of.

For example, in the late 1980s the price of acrylates was very high, with only three suppliers (two European and one US) who appeared to enjoy a remarkable similarity of pricing. The Japanese and Koreans then decided to enter this market and import to the UK. The local suppliers were very nervous. They had the belief that there really was product starting to be imported and prices began to fall. One sales person asked if a company was buying 'from the East'. The answer he got contained two correct statements: 'Yes, it comes a long way across the water and it is from an eastern port.' He left convinced that he needed to match prices on large volumes. In fact Houston, Texas is an eastern port of the US and it is a long way across the water from Teesside . . .

This example also contains a key negotiating fault on behalf of the sales person, namely not asking direct and simple questions, which will be covered as a skill later in the chapter.

The second 'truthless tactic' is boldly to answer the question, only not the one you were asked. So to the question 'Are you buying from the East?' the answer is 'Frankly we both know that, yes, we simply have to buy from the most cost-effective sources however far away they are.'

Once again, there is no lie in this statement, although if the word 'yes' can be fitted into the answer to simply act as a connector, it has a powerful reinforcing effect. If, of course, you take the definition of lying to be 'deliberately leading someone to believe something that is wrong', then both the above tactics will count as lies. The real issue is that there is no guessing what the other side is actually hearing from you, and all really good negotiators would not let such statements go without further clarification.

Careful listening is a greatly under-used negotiating skill, which is fortunate for those of us who genuinely don't want to lie, but for whom the bare truth may prove unhelpful. Sales people have for a long time had the legal back-up of 'caveat emptor' (buyer beware) and there is no reason why this should not be reflected in the reverse. Buying in business is a professional game and as such professionals will use all the tactics they can to take advantage.

Keep them waiting

Another time-honoured tactic is to let the other side sweat in reception for a bit in order to show them who calls the tune. In a busy world this is probably done more by default than design: many departments are at lean levels and you may have to keep the other team waiting as you dash from one meeting to the next.

Nevertheless, it should rarely be used as a tactic. First, most sales people don't 'sweat' in reception, waiting merely gives them the opportunity to do the preparation that they should have done before. The good ones use the time to pick up more information, perhaps from company magazines, the receptionist, the visitors' book, or simply from hearing more of the chat that goes on in these places. If it's done by default then that means you have started the negotiation off in the worst possible state by putting pressure on yourself, while the other side has had a pleasant moment of quiet contemplation to marshal their arguments.

Interruptions – especially by the phone – are also ways to keep people waiting, albeit during the meeting. Again this is something that many buyers do by default, and it is an appalling piece of positioning. It takes up time on one task that should have been planned for another, inappropriate information can be given away as you discuss matters with other people, and it gives the opposition useful time to plan their next move.

Sharp attention to the detail of time gives strong signals to others that you are in control of your side of the ship. It will engender respect, as well as ensuring that you have the right amount of time to prepare yourself for the discussion.

Acceptable dirty tricks

There is a point of view that some dirty tricks fall into the category of skilful tactics and it is after all a professional game we are playing. Footballers do take the occasional 'dive' and in rugby the referee is not called in 'because he hurt me'. Perhaps, therefore, it is acceptable to appear to be in a dreadful muddle about the figures, feigning confusion and awaiting your moment to ask the innocent 'killer question'. It could be that in a group negotiation you all have each other's mobile numbers pre-dialled into your phones, so that if any of you senses that the others need some time out you can give them a quick call from your pocket. It could even be as simple as the classic 'good cop/bad cop' routine.

These can all be useful, and sometimes they can actually bring some fun to the process of negotiation. The question to consider is whether they really are the best ways to achieve your outcome. If you need time out in a negotiation it is possible simply to ask. If you are pretending to be simple-minded about the figures, will this affect the supplier's desire to offer more subtle forms of savings? It is easy to see such tactics as being wrong, but it is also easy to become too pious. Commercial interaction should not be sterile, it should be fun, interesting, challenging and stimulating – and the appropriate use of the occasional tactical move can help make it more so.

Simple skills: The golden triangle of negotiating success

There is a sweet spot where deals are always struck. This point is at the place where the three forces at play within any negotiation have all been given due attention (Figure 6.3).

The triangle of their intersection is a great place to be. Yet far too much time is spent simply in the factual sector, where people assume that because it is a business deal the facts of the matter will define the result. However, facts are surprisingly fragile and flexible; they are rarely enough to form a good deal. If they were we would not need sales forces

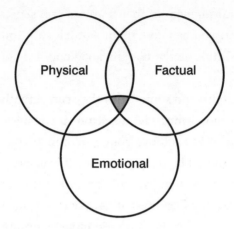

Figure 6.3

and buying departments, we could leave it simply to the accountants and administrators. To help avoid this nightmarish vision, for each of these forces there are some easy rules to help generate success.

Physical

The influence and connection between the physical state you are in and the way you think are increasingly well established. The reverse process – thinking to physical – has been proven since Pavlov, although ringing bells until your suppliers salivate in anticipation of the deal is probably taking things a bit far.

The key point here is to pay attention to it. You may not be able to judge a book fully by its cover, but it will give you an indication of the contents. How your office is laid out, how you dress, how you sit and how you talk will all have a significant impact on the way you come across. There are plenty of mistakes that can be made in interpretation, of course: you may fold your arms because you are cold, not because you are defensive. Do you sense uneasiness in the other party because of the solution you have suggested or do they just have a bad back?

While paying attention to the physical details of the other party is critical, overly interpreting them – at least consciously – can be dangerous. What is far more important is to keep in control of those things you can be sure about: the way you look, the way you feel, the way you sit and talk. These are things that even a small amount of attention will help to be more effective. It may be as impish as wearing the competition's tie and using a pen with their logo during the meeting, it may be as detailed as creating a real oasis of physical preparation prior to a meeting. Even if the other party is not as sophisticated in their approach, they will certainly subconsciously pick up the appropriate messages, and this is by far the most effective way to influence them.

Controlling the physical space is also important, both in terms of the third dimension (i.e. the room you are in) and the fourth dimension, time. If you are negotiating on your own patch then your choice of office or meeting room, reception area or restaurant needs to be positively made. One critical piece of experience is that sales people are far less likely to give the best deal when they believe that others are listening.

An experienced buyer from marine sealant company Fosroc Expandite shared his office with his deputy buyer. It was a long office, with one desk facing the door from the left and one further down opposite the door. When you were seated the other desk was always behind you and to one side; the buyers could see each other but you could not see them both at once. This is very effective for unnerving people, especially if both occasionally make comments. However, sales people will feel unsettled and may not give all they can, preferring to put off a decision that could have been concluded at that meeting.

You can always have some influence over space, even if it is not your territory. The skill is to have the courage to ask for any moves you want at the earliest moment. In the above example, a skilled negotiator should 'call it' – openly raise the issue they feel uncomfortable about – the moment they sit down. It is critical not to assign blame: this desk arrangement may be deliberate, but it might also be the only way they could plug their computers into the wall sockets; perhaps the other party genuinely did not know that the chair you are in has a broken base with a sharp piece of plastic poking into your back.

In this instance to 'call it' would be to make a statement that is factual, open and only concerns your own feelings: 'Actually I find it difficult sitting in this position. I want to be able to talk to you both and it is hard for my back to keep turning around. Could I move my chair next to you so I don't have to twist?' If at the same time you actually start to make the move, it is very difficult to resist; and if they do say no, it tells you a lot about the conscious tactics they are prepared to adopt. The one other critical thing is to keep your mind clear of any thoughts of retaliation. As will be explained in the next section, if having moved your chair you are thinking 'Hah! That got you, matey', the negotiation is going to go downhill from that moment.

Whatever the physical impact that you find difficult, from a crushing handshake to the fact that the room has got too stuffy to concentrate, always call it, and always call it early.

Factual

Many facts are not absolute, they are simply one way of looking at things. An interesting acid test when negotiating is to realize that if you are in negotiation, then by definition both parties do not know all the facts. If they did there would be no negotiation, as the result would be self-evident.

There was a dispute between the chemical groups ICI and Huels. The latter's service to a Teesside plant was very poor, with many deliveries made late, and Huels was downrated on supplier performance. Its initial response was dismay: it could clearly see the facts that it had a 99% delivery rate across the UK that was On-Time-In-Full (OTIF). However, the Teesside plant rated it at 67%. Of course, both sides were right: over the many thousands of deliveries in the UK overall Huels performed well, but it just so happened that many of the 1% that were late were concentrated on Teesside, where the requirement for an offloading pump meant that drivers did not allow enough time to rig this up prior to delivery.

Even with a relatively simple problem like this, the facts that each side was looking at were not the same – and yet they were from the same data set. This also brings in the concept of 'facts conditioning'. This is the process whereby individuals will delete or distort information based on experience. Many people have some good experience of a supplier, perhaps a shop or restaurant, and will say they always get good service. Only if you press them will they admit that the occasional error does occur, but they overlook it. Conversely, if you think your builder is lazy or trains never arrive on time, you may ignore moments of good work or timely arrival. The actual facts are not looked at, people form a perception of them and this perception is their reality, regardless of what actually happened.

The key skill is first to realize your own distortions and check that they have not given you a selective view of the facts. Secondly, be open to the perceptions of others. Restating the facts to them will not change their minds, you have to tackle their perceptions and only then will you start to make progress.

Lastly, there is a connection between the facts and win–win. It is tempting when reporting the facts inside the organization to show how skilful negotiation reduced the seller's price and totalled a saving of over £100 000. This may well be true when comparing the price to alternative quotes and taking the volume over two years.

However, it is also important to help the other side save as much face as they can, to give them something that they could report within their organization showing that they too have done a good job. Many negotiators believe that should be up to the other party to sort out – it's not my job to cover for him. The more you can help the other side the more they will be able to believe they have a good deal, and this will help them look at the facts differently next time too.

Emotional

Emotion is certainly something that plays strongly in negotiations. Some believe that passion for the result or anger at a problem are unhelpful emotions that cloud the facts and cause problems. While this may well be true, they are ignored at great peril: they need to be understood and worked with to ensure a positive outcome.

A simple framework to work with is to consider first the way in which you manage your emotions in approaching others, and secondly how you manage your emotions in reacting to others.

The skills in this area can be very practical. You don't need to hug trees for a week and seek your inner self – although this might help – but most people don't have the time for it before most negotiations. The biggest challenge is to avoid being in the wrong mood. This could be because you have been annoyed by the stance the other party has taken, or it could be because your one-year-old chose to be sick on your work suit just as you were leaving the house for nursery.

Both of these events will cloud your judgement, both will leave thoughts around your head that will leak out and could easily give the wrong impression. A great deal of research tells us that over 60% of communication is done non-verbally (Figure 6.4).

The actual process for this communication is in micro-movements and effects on tonality that are picked up by others subconsciously. Hence if you have not been open about 'calling' a tactic and believe you have just scored a point, it will come through and will cause the other side to react

Communication

Figure 6.4

against it. Even if your irritation is based on a fact separate from the negotiation, you will still send off signals that show concern and the opposition will not be able to mind read that they are not in fact related to the negotiation.

Managing these emotions is therefore a useful skill and the ABC of doing this is a good method to use (Figure 6.5). The great thing about this triangle is that you can enter it at any corner and it will start to have a positive effect.

Arousal is using external stimuli to help change your mood. If you are stuck in traffic you could turn on the radio or a CD, if you have been in front of the computer all morning before the others arrive then go outside and get some fresh air in your lungs.

Behaviour is using your own internal stimulus: this could be breathing more deeply or taking a couple of flights of stairs at a pace to get the

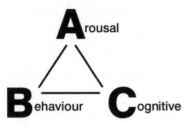

Figure 6.5

blood going. One behaviour that genuinely changes moods is singing – it may sound bizarre, but joyously humming your way to the meeting room has quite a marked effect on the opposition.

Lastly, you can actually think yourself into a better mood, using your cognitive skills. Moods in fact only occur in the brain, so it is only here that you are going to be able to change them. You always have a choice of mood. It may not feel like it when you are stressed and hassled, but there is always a choice. Any of the ABC mechanisms can be used to put you in the right frame of mind, whether that be relaxed, concerned or even raging with anger. As long as you have chosen this mood as being effective for your outcome, it is the right mood to be in.

This ABC can also be used in reacting to others. If you do find that you have reacted with antagonism to a proposal someone has just made, perhaps it is time to take a break, have a glass of water, take a walk in the car park. Likewise, if you find yourself with blinkered thinking – 'She is only saying that to get at me' – challenge yourself cognitively – 'Can I think differently about her intentions?'

Any reaction starts with our most effective early warning system, gut feel. The great thing about gut feel is that it never fails to sense that something is going wrong; the problem is that it almost never tells you what exactly it is, it merely flags an issue. In many negotiations that fail you will find that people sensed they were going nowhere long before they actually collapsed. Once again the skill is to call it, to raise openly that you sense things have gone off track, or to check your concerns that the other side appears to have become angry about something. You are not saying that they are angry, simply that you are interpreting their mood that way and is this correct?

Emotions are a vital part of all negotiations and the more they can be embraced, managed and developed, the more likely you are to be successful in every deal you make.

Concluding thoughts

Much mystique surrounds the world of negotiating. It is particularly unhelpful to imbue people in buying roles with magical powers. This often results in buyers being brought in very late to an already existing deal. They are then expected to work miracles on the price when most of the options have already been given away. Furthermore, this belief in mystic powers often means that buyers get their own development needs in negotiating overlooked. They may do it every day, but playing even a lot of games with amateurs doesn't make you a professional.

There has been a move towards pushing for win–win relationships and taking a step back from the more traditional 'table-thumping' approach of buying legends of old. It is true that win–win solutions were fairly novel ten years ago, but not all situations allow for such deals. It is simply one of several types of stance that can be taken ranging between passive, aggressive and partnership. However, words such as trust and partnership are often over-used and employed in the wrong context.

Whichever is the chosen approach – mostly relying on market positions – if all three of the factual, physical and emotional aspects of the deal are properly considered, then there will be a good result.

Negotiation is a skill – it can be taught, it can be practised. As long as it is respected for what it is, a practical method to achieve your business goals, then the mystique can fall away and buyers and sellers can get on with their work.

7
Measuring Performance

MEASURING PERFORMANCE IS A FASCINATING TOPIC AND IT HAS been around in business for many years. Profit (and loss) were always key business tenets and, with the exception of certain large US accountancy and power firms, were generally accepted as the sacred icons of measurement.

The advent of gurus such as William Edwards Deming and Philip Crosby in the 1970s started a trend for wider measures. They moved quality assurance and control processes from purely engineering concepts into a wider business context. In the 1980s and 1990s many companies chased British Standards and ISO quality registrations and the whole area of quality assurance and quality control generated a measuring frenzy throughout the business world. Each department had to have a variety of 'control graphs' prominently on display, and a complete new language developed concerning 'variance analyses' and 'statistical significance'.

Some say this led to 'analysis paralysis' where a warehouse stuffed full of product one month was a 'rogue data point' and a three-month drop in sales could be 'seasonal variation only'. A new algebraic equation was born:

$$NR + CSE = R$$

NR = Non Result
CSE = Convincing Statistical Explanation
R = Result

The days of having a graph on every wall may have passed – the good news is that this doesn't matter. First, the only graphs that ever got pinned anywhere were the good ones. Second, if you had a bad one, then simple recalibration, judicious choice of starting date and the use of logarithmic scaling for particularly alarming drops or peaks could still make the graph look good. They were often only used as defensive justification and, if they were actually of real importance, they unwittingly provided helpful insight for visiting reps into where your weak points were.

There is a great quote from Einstein on this issue, and he should know a thing or two about measurement: 'Not everything that can be counted counts, and not everything that counts can be counted.'

Purchasing is on the horns of a classic dilemma. If it makes major claims of savings, they may simply be discounted. If it quietly gets on and 'does the right thing', it can be sidelined in the business. Showing how savings you have achieved make it to the bottom line is thought to be difficult, as is striking a balance between short-term price gains and long-term efficiency savings.

This chapter will first look at the question of 'Why measure?', then move to look at what should be measured, especially with regard to the range of harder and softer measures. Analysing when you should use these and how to make them tools of lasting value will also be explained.

Why measure?

A good part of the measurement bonanza that went on was driven by the philosophy that 'if you can't measure it you can't improve it'. This became quite a strong feeling in many businesses. 'Process improvement' teams were born and for a short time were slightly more feared than the Stasi police.

'Why measure?' is a really important question if you are to be successful in improving what you do. From this it will drive what you want to measure and, perhaps more importantly, what you can stop having to waste time measuring. If you catch yourself frantically getting graphs together because you have a process improvement team meeting on Tuesday, then it really is time to sit back and ask 'Why?'.

There are several reasons to measure, and segmenting what you do, or want to do, into each of these can be helpful.

- *Defensive*: to show you were right and something should stop being done.
- *Justification*: to show that something needs to be done.

- *Improvement*: to look for the reason for a problem.
- *Control*: a running measure to look for minor adjustments.
- *Efficiency*: to look for activity that can be cut out.
- *Effectiveness*: to measure the impact you can have on the bottom line.

There is nothing wrong with any of these reasons to measure: sometimes you need to defend your corner or justify a difficult decision. This segmentation is important to avoid measuring the wrong thing – or at least to avoid presenting the results in the wrong way.

This approach of looking at the core reason behind the measure can also help avoid needless measures, even though they may be born of good intent. At PZ Cussons (PZC) in Manchester, the procurement groups wanted to measure their suppliers' On-Time-In-Full (OTIF) delivery – essentially a sensible thing to do. Production does have its variances (!) and on many occasions the allocated slot time for deliveries has to be changed. The logistics group at PZC liaised with suppliers and deliveries were often put back against the original plan to allow for tight stock control. When the 'actual' delivery was entered against the plan, however, it then showed up as late. The only way to amend this was via a complicated set of phone calls to re-enter the due date so that the delivery date matched.

The real issue here is that the 'Why?' behind OTIF measures is to ensure that suppliers are delivering when needed. Recording the delivery as late, when in fact the suppliers were showing remarkable flexibility, was not helping PZC to realize which were good and which were poor suppliers.

A simple measure change helped this. They took the bold step to assume that all suppliers were OTIF. The plant knew if suppliers were causing a problem, and if they were, the procurement groups started to enter the data again. This shift from measuring everything to only measuring when there was a problem helped to give them both more time and more accurate data.

The last thought on 'Why?' is very closely associated to the issue of 'Who for?'. One of the golden rules of measurement is that the person doing the measuring must have some sort of interest in the results. Interest in this context means a tangible outcome, and hopefully a positive one. Empowering turkeys to measure their own body-weight growth curve in the lead-up to Christmas may not get you the most accurate of results.

This is surprisingly often overlooked and the pressures can be quite subtle. In one supply chain the buyers were asked to measure raw material 'stock-outs'; that is, when there was insufficient product to run the lines. However, the buyers were only targeted on the stock-outs, not on the stock levels, which were a target for the logistics group. The buyers did not want to look bad on their measure and they wanted to strike good deals. On this basis they negotiated high 'bulk discounts'. This meant that they could protect themselves with large buffer stocks and succeed in their own measure, at the same time providing a real headache for the logistics group's measures. They all worked for the same supply chain and had good intent, but local pressures often supersede the 'greater good'. The reason for measurement needs to be uniform throughout the supply chain.

What to measure?

Before reaching for the toolbox of measures, two factors will help you choose which tools to use: first, where you are in your development cycle; and second, how 'hard' or 'soft' the data is that you are measuring. The concept of measuring different things at different points in a cycle is true for other types of functions such as marketing, and it is true in life as well. If you are a poor golfer then you measure your success by how many balls you lost; if you are better then you measure how many shots you took. In purchasing you can hold a variety of stages of maturity of relationship with suppliers. You could have a mature relationship with

Stage of development	Object	Performance measure
1. Flat pricing	Contain price	Performance against last month/year price
2. Total cost focus	Contain cost over total product life	1. Process activity mapping 2. Production variety mix 3. Decisions point analysis 4. Cost transparency
3. Supply-side management	To gain from suppliers their specialist expertise and skill	1. Communication analysis 2. Supplier development matrix 3. Quality function deployment
4. Strategic sourcing	Work jointly with suppliers to increase value in chain	1. Supply chain response matrix 2. Total time maps
5. Networking and relationship management	Improve total understanding and mutual network development	1. Value stream mapping 2. Advance communications analysis

Figure 7.1

one commodity and be really feeling your way in another area that is new to R&D.

Figure 7.1 is an overview of the various stages of development and the types of things that you could be looking to measure. Within any of these areas there is the second issue, which is the spectrum of savings types. Some savings could be described as hard: you are measuring money that in some way hits the bottom line. Some are still tangible but may add value or give options for savings – these are slightly softer. Lastly there are measurements for the truly softer benefits that are increasingly being seen as the real enablers of improved performance.

Tools to measure the hard stuff

One company once carefully added up all the savings claims it had made over the previous five years. It came to 104% of its total spend – which did rather call into question the problem of how savings do actually make it to the bottom line. The following examples show how hard measurement can be.

- On average my staff cost £30 000 p.a. I have just negotiated a deal that will save 15% of five people's time – how much have I saved?
- I have just negotiated the hire-car rate down from £27 per day to £24 per day – how much have I saved?
- I have just negotiated down the 17% increase in price that the supplier wanted to 8% – how much have I saved?

These are questions that a lot of buyers face. Even if you had all of the surrounding data it might not help. Take the second example. Last year we bought 4200 'car days' from our hire-car partner and our business is expected to be steady for this year. Does that mean that I have saved £12 600?

In reality this saving may well not make it to the 'bottom line'. Each department usually controls its own travel budget and is challenged to keep within that. If you have made hire cars cheaper that is good, but there is nothing to stop people simply spending that saving elsewhere. They may hire more cars and visit more customers – that could generate extra earnings, but no actual savings. Worse still, they might simply spend it on an extra beer one night in the hotel.

One approach is to focus on where the money actually goes. It is possible to measure this, and you can then claim the real benefits when you can trace it through to its final destination. A method that proved to work well in ICI was to look at savings in three ways that relate to the increasingly softer nature of the impact:

- *Bottom-line impact*: hard savings that clearly hit the balance sheet.
- *Rate options*: savings such as hire-car rates, or hotel rooms where a day rate is lowered.
- *Cost avoidance*: where you have lessened the effects of an increase and you can also record efficiency improvements under this heading.

Interestingly, this can be looked at for both positive and negative movements, which is a way not only to get a realistic picture for the company, but also to avoid credibility problems regarding the claims you make. If you only count savings, people rapidly discount your data.

Bottom-line impact

There are some simple rules that make this effective:

- *Is it cheaper/dearer than last year?* Many products are purchased year on year, so this often covers the bulk of purchases. Set a unit price and simply measure against that on a calendar basis.
- *Record positives and negatives.* Negatives are often ignored in many companies, which is plain stupid. Even if you are dealing in a real commodity, where the world price goes up and down beyond your control, it is important to know what is going on. The graph can look quite tough sometimes, although strangely enough once you have shown it to others in the business your credibility rating shoots up. If through clever timing of purchases you have avoided some of the major price spikes, this is recorded as 'cost avoidance'.
- *Simple volume/value multiplier.* No need to make it complicated: if you saved £10 per unit and you buy 1000 units, then you saved £10 000.
- *Forward estimate and check back.* Budgeting and forecasting are always in vogue. Simply estimate your volume offtake for the year, and then check your savings claims against actuals as they come in. This may mean that your claims vary over the year – and so they should. Plenty of departments have claimed deals 'worth a million' while quietly forgetting that the product line in question was overstocked and then withdrawn. Again, you get the classic credibility gap when purchasing claims a success and yet the business has dismal results.

- *Inflation ignored.* This could be a question of your own accounting conventions. However, it pushes you towards harder reality when making savings claims, which is never a bad thing.

Rate options

Here are a few guidelines and one golden rule:

- *Select units by common sense.* Typically these are on unit items with a fairly variable rate of purchase volume. They should also be items where the user can 'spend the difference'. Hire cars and hotel room rates are good examples. Consultancy may be one as well. For a project you could have £50 000 allocated to IT consultancy support. If you have just agreed a drop in your preferred supplier by £100 per day, is this a saving? Probably not: you will find that your IT manager has found a little extra top-up project to take up the slack.

- *Can be positive or negative.* As with all real measurements, you have to record situations where the price has gone up – although again, check against volumes purchased. Before you worry about having to accept the 10% increase from your advertising agent, you could check against the real volume purchased. Those who use the service may well have voted with their feet and decided not to use that particular design agency any more because of the cost.

- *Estimated against last year's usage.* As above, do annual calculations and adjust as the year goes on.

- *The golden rule of claiming.* You can only claim these as savings if total fixed costs for the relevant area are under budget by the proposed savings. This is a tough rule, and probably a good one. If you believe that you have negotiated the potential to save manufacturing £100 000, then if it is 'on budget' where have the savings gone? If handled with appropriate care for impact, this can be a very powerful set of data to get real engagement at a senior level. It is particularly effective at controlling maverick or 'pet' buying habits. These are where users ignore your better deals in favour of someone they prefer, or are simply too lazy to make the changes you have suggested.

Cost avoidance

This area is most likely to come into play when you either have commodities where the market price is realistically out of your control, or suppliers are still in the habit of the infamous annual price-increase letter. It is also an effective way to measure efficiency improvements, which are an important topic in their own right and are separately explained below.

The guidelines are as follows:

- *Split the benefit from the burden.* If a supplier comes with a 7% rise and you manage to beat it down to 3%, record the 3% increase as a 'negative bottom line' result. Record the 4% 'saving' you made as cost avoidance.
- *Only count 50% of savings against new product purchases.* Perhaps a harsh rule; again, what is important is to be realistic. This means that if you are buying some new item, possibly even capital equipment, you can argue that the price you eventually agree is in fact the market price. The fact that the supplier started at 20% higher

may just have been a stance, not a real saving. On the other hand, if professional buyers were not in place perhaps you would not have got such a good deal. Taking only half the benefit helps to allow for both these factors.

• *Can be a way to record working capital savings.* Lowering stock levels is a classic purchasing activity. This can be done through a variety of methods, from total outsourcing in terms of consignment stock to simple improved lead times. The challenge is to record these savings accurately. They are usually only one-offs and it is tempting to record them as a bottom line impact. It is certainly true that they do have a very hard effect on the bottom line. Purchasing departments often suffer from the annual 'silly season' where financial pressures dictate a massive destock. This of course goes straight to the bottom line, savings are claimed for the year end, and the next three months' production gets messed up through a lack of product. However, you have only really avoided the cost for a short time, and even with consignment stock the saving is a one-off. Recording it as 'cost avoidance' probably gives it the status it really deserves.

Tools to measure the softer efficiency improvements

Product

Measuring efficiency improvements, like many other measures, is something that you can make very easy – and you can also make it horribly complicated.

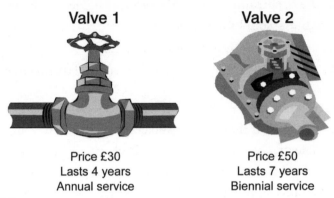

Valve 1

Price £30
Lasts 4 years
Annual service

Valve 2

Price £50
Lasts 7 years
Biennial service

Figure 7.2

First, this is not a science. You will need to make a range of subjective judgements and be confident in seeing them through.

Take the example of a negotiated deal where you have decided to buy valve 1 instead of valve 2 (Figure 7.2). If you have 400 pumps in total and buy 100 replacements of these a year, there are some interesting calculations you can make and probably only one real fact of which you can be sure: a budget overspend this year of £2000.

On the other hand, if an average service costs £50, then you can do a calculation of increased price less volume purchased and lower service costs – net effect £48 000 saved over six years.

Savings calculations like this can take you on a journey of ever-increasing complexity. Consider the following factors:

• How much does it cost to service?

- What is the opportunity cost of the service engineers, i.e. what other valuable things could they be doing?
- What are the savings from fewer transactions?
- How do we know the new pumps will actually last seven years?

This is where efficiency savings require bold decisions and they may have to be subjective. If they are not subjective, at least they are going to need to be selectively objective. Going back to the questions, 'Why measure?' is a useful yardstick here. If you need to justify the decision to improve the quality of pumps, £48 000 is going to be pretty helpful. It is still an estimated figure, and with rapidly changing business and job situations it will be extraordinary if you can look back after six years and prove that you were right. Even if you can, are you really going to boast to your colleagues that you made a decision that long ago that has just proved to be a good one?

People

The key success to measurement in this area is 'usability'.

Concorde made its last flight in 2003 and it was a great example of how apparent leaps forward in technology don't always yield the efficiency benefits they claim. It did cut the flight time by 50%. In reality, over the total travel time (New York city centre to London city centre), the saving was probably more like 20%. If you then add in the fact that Concorde was a daytime flight, compared to the usual 'red-eye' overnight flights, the picture changes again. In practice, Concorde flights took up the best part of a whole working day, whereas if you flew overnight you not only got two whole work days, you could appear in the London office very early and claim 100 macho management points.

This concept is critical when thinking how to measure time savings through efficiency. It is very unusual to find anyone in business who claims to be under-worked. Most people state that they are operating at 120%, perhaps even more. If you reduce lead times or streamline a procedure that takes 15% out of a job task, you need to know where the benefit is going to occur. You could find that the individual is less stressed and has a better work–life balance, which is admirable and sensible. It is also a very difficult measurement to claim as part of a case for making changes.

Some major changes do result in job losses. Outsourcing call centres to India has become rather fashionable. The numbers are very alluring: a graduate employee for only 10% of the salary charged in the UK. These are no doubt savings that are being fully calculated and add up to a significant figure. At the same time, you hear through the news and company reports comments such as: 'We hope to be able to re-deploy the bulk of our employees in other areas'. If that is so, calculating the real net saving becomes very messy.

A simple approach is to take all of these as 'cost avoidance' and not try too hard to make the benefits actually traceable through to the balance sheet. Recording the various efficiency claims is important, as it provides useful management information to help shape staff options for the future and when considering 'up-shifting' skills away from more manual tasks.

Hard measurement in this area may yield low returns and may get you into the ironic position of wasting expensive management time trying to calculate the time you have saved in other areas.

Tools to measure the truly soft stuff

In this context, what are called 'soft skills' cover a broad range from emotional intelligence (EI) to desired attitudinal approaches. EI is that set of skills that encompass high self-awareness, mood management, self-motivation and interpersonal expertise.

Attitudinal approaches are usually high-level descriptors of behaviour that the company would like its employees to adopt. The Abbey Life group adopted high-level statements such as 'Of your world' and 'Always now', ICI used such phrases as 'Can do' and 'Results focused'. Beneath these lie a larger set of definitions that would spell out what the behaviour would look like when you saw it.

To call such skills, attitudes and abilities 'soft' is somewhat daft. Not only are they among the most potent and powerful skills in negotiation, they are also among the hardest skills to have the courage to develop. It would be far better if they were defined as 'impact skills'. It is easy enough to read a book on developing contract skills or outsourcing expertise. It is far more of a challenge to work on your ability to manage your mood during a tricky debate with some fool from production who has just changed the buying requirements for the fourth time this week.

Controlling the impact that you have in this circumstance is a really hard task and could not be described as a soft skill at all.

The success in measuring these skills again lies in realizing that this is going to have to be subjective, so don't worry about exact definitions. It is also an area where the targets only need to show relative improvement. If you are measuring more standard factors such as OTIF then you can aim for a hard figure – say 98% OTIF, or stock can be measured exactly to an end target of 'three days' cover'. Impact skills do not have an end point that can be measured, only a relative movement from where you started.

Word models are the best way to measure them. Take the high-level definition and drill down to a set of behaviours that you can see. It also helps to use the measure of how often these behaviours are displayed as an easy way to define between different levels of achievement.

For example, the attitude could be 'challenges constructively' and the next level down described as 'always thinks of new and innovative ways to tackle problems and puts them into effect' (Figure 7.3). These can be

Level score	1	2	3	4	5
Behaviour	Is interested in new ideas and will support them if raised by others	Shows imagination in dealing with problems	Challenges thinking from time to time, and occasionally pushes ideas through to effect	Often challenges others to good effect, with occasional alienation	Regularly challenges accepted norms in a positive and engaging style with positive effects

Figure 7.3

scored by the individual and the manager, and then compared. The most valuable part of this type of measurement almost certainly comes in the discussion. It doesn't really matter if there are different viewpoints or that the facts behind the scores are hard to verify. The important outcome is that individuals know the attitude is going to be looked at and they have some idea of what they need to do differently to improve. Measurement in this area is more a delivery vehicle for development than a monitor of its success.

Impact skills *can* therefore be measured. It is even possible over time for some more objective criteria to be produced as increased experience improves the descriptors.

Measuring supplier performance

One of the issues that is continually under review is the topic of how you measure the performance of your suppliers. This is clearly an important area, but it is not rocket science – the skill is to keep it simple and build on others' experience before reinventing the wheel. The three questions to consider are closely linked: why are you measuring them, how should you measure them and what are you measuring?

In considering 'Why?' an early issue to sort out is whether the measurement is part of a selection process or part of an improvement process. The potential depth, breadth and length of measurement will vary depending on this, and need to be resourced accordingly. A selection process can be more one-off and may well involve quite a wide variety of parameters. The data needs to be hard; that is, commentary and opinions are difficult to make relative selections against.

An improvement process, on the other hand, needs to last – by definition it should run over a period of time so that gains can be monitored. There is wide experience showing that lasting measures need to be simple, with the data easy to collect on a regular basis. Larger corporations are littered with improvement measures that are unused because they are too complicated and perfection has become the enemy of the practical and good. Improvement measures can also cope more effectively with opinion or softer data; indeed, it is often this that provides insights into where new improvements can be found.

How to measure is linked to why. A selection process, because it is one-off, could be coordinated via anything from an expensive database to the back of an envelope, and provided that the criteria are clear, it will work. Improvement measures require more thought. One big problem has been over-emphasis on automation and systems, where there is a misconception that they can help. This has led to complicated processes and everything becoming very impersonal, with those who have to input the data losing sight and sense of why they are bothering to do it.

Supplier performance information is a critical piece of a buyer's knowledge: it goes to the very core of negotiating better service and better deals. Despite this, many buyers shy away from putting real hours into collecting data. They want it to be automated, collated and delivered in summary form. This is an efficiency to be challenged. The very process of seeking data gets the buyers into contact with key players, it shows that they care, and it allows for softer data to be explored, verified and quantified. It is a job worth investing real time in.

What to measure is purely situational. Even such apparently basic factors such as OTIF may not be relevant in certain circumstances. The key is to chase the money: look at the levers in your own circumstances and map out where the benefits can be realized. In addition to looking for your own money levers, seek the same information from your suppliers. Buyers can get tied up in their internal world, so asking suppliers what would be worth measuring can reveal issues that concern them and in turn could yield benefits.

There are probably more supplier measurement processes in the world than there are suppliers. Every company wants to invent their own; even if they have one, they probably feel that they should reinvent it because the old one has fallen by the wayside. Keeping it simple, keeping it personal and keeping it driven and resourced from within purchasing can help provide real data, and save more wheels from reinvention.

Measures that last

It is a real challenge to find any business organization, strategy or initiative that runs for a good length of time. There is a widely held belief that businesses must continually 'adapt or die' in a fast-moving marketplace. There is no doubt that some markets are developing quickly. There is also no doubt that many business leaders confuse movement with action. Constant reorganization and restructuring make it difficult to measure any element of transactions without the goal posts being shifted.

There are some key points that have proved useful for some companies in helping measures to be effective – although they may not be what you are expecting.

First, break all the rules

- *The highest-level backing.* There is a belief that you need high-level backing to make something last. Beware of this two-edged sword. Measurement is something that needs to be carried out at the coal face. Strategy and culture can be supported from on high, but measurement needs to be backed by those who do it.
- *Central reporting in common formats.* Collating measures at some higher level will be needed if you are to see wider trends, or you are operating over a number of units that have to be coordinated. You also need to avoid the 'head office reporting syndrome'. This drives people to unnecessary work in changing formats. Timing is rarely relevant for the users of the measure and can lead to a form-filling mentality.
- *Report the monetary savings.* It is understandable that if you are running a business you want to see the financial effect that a range of activities is having. Beware the temptation to force all measures back to a monetary value, however. This can drive local behaviour the wrong way. If you are simply reporting savings, it makes higher price/

lower overall cost purchases unattractive to negotiate. It also tempts people to ignore globally driven commodity price movements. Lastly, some of the most important measures could be on impact skills, and these do not lend themselves easily to short-term monetary reporting.

Then make it relevant

- *Data collection by users.* With modern IT systems a high degree of automation in data collection is always possible. There are some obvious efficiency benefits from this, as well as missed opportunities. Computers are stupid, they don't think, they just 'do'. If there is always some small human intervention as the data is collected there is a far greater chance that issues will be noticed sooner.

- *Put the work into context.* Above all else this is critical. If the measure is meaningful to the individual who is taking it, it will be carried out properly. Measurement, particularly on a regular basis, is often delegated to more administrative staff. This not only leads to crazy data – somebody entering 2 tonnes instead of 2 kilos – it is also missing the chance to see the real action point of your decisions. If you actually go down to goods inwards occasionally to measure OTIF, it can be enlightening to see drivers stacked up the road or piles of stock spilling over into the yard.

- *People with both the tools and the attitude.* For measures to last there need to be simple and reliable methods for collecting data. One warehouse for plastic goods in London had a fancy new computer system put in to record stock. Needless to say it did not run very well early on, and the centralized format for records made it hard to use. On two occasions stock errors were reported by the warehouse staff to head office, but initially they were not believed. 'Our system shows you do have the stock,' said head office. 'Yes, and our chalk marks on the wall show we don't.' No prizes for guessing who was right. The attitude of purchasing people is also a factor worth nurturing. Purchasing tends to have a slightly higher proportion of technically or transaction-minded staff, which is an advantage in measurement. There is a trend to employ more strategically minded buyers. This will have its advantages for wider thinking, but beware its effect on completion and finishing skills.

Concluding thoughts

Measures can be tempting: if you make enough of them you can probably find one that backs your point of view, and they can give the excellent appearance of being in control of the situation.

They can also be a massive waste of effort. The key point is always to check why you are measuring: what is the point of it and has the world moved on since you last asked?

Set yourself some clear categories of measurement that everyone can use and have some house rules. These are particularly important where you have several teams or locations and you want to make fair comparisons.

It is possible to measure 'personal impact' type skills. In this area it is a relative movement you are looking for; it can be jointly subjective; and half of the benefit comes from going through the process itself, rather than focusing on the number you agree at the end.

Most measures fail because of simple human factors. People don't know why they are conducting them so they make mistakes, or become resentful because they are bored reporting to the centre. Then a new manager takes over, or the organization changes and you start with a new set of criteria. The more the 'measurers' can see the results of their labour, the more value you are likely to gain from it.

8
E-commerce

THE E-COMMERCE SHOW WAS GOING TO TRANSFORM EVERYTHING. It was going to be the brightest star on business Broadway. From the early days of consumer-hype sites the pundits predicted that it was the tiny start of a massive change – as the showbiz phrase goes: 'You ain't seen nothing yet!'

How true. Several years on and many in mainstream business-to-business companies are still waiting for something to happen. The initial costs have sometimes proved expensive, the benefits have been unclear, and businesses have not embraced the total change of processes and systems that is needed to make these things work well.

However, there has been quite enough jaundiced writing about this subject. E-commerce is a great tool if you know how to use it, and there are real benefits to be gained. So the really interesting question is not so much 'What can it do?' but more 'How and where might it be successful?'

Here is a simple analogy that helps answer the above question.

The E-Plan diet

The world of e-commerce is very much like a diet:

- If you absolutely follow the logic it works.
- If you play at it you fail.
- Some parts of it suit some individuals better than others.
- Announcing it loudly is not going to get results.
- Following it through grinding reality will work.
- Everyone has a horror story.
- Some people pay a fortune and stay fat, others can get thin on very little expense.
- You have always heard of someone else having astounding success, but never actually been able to meet anyone who has.

The tough lesson that has to be learned is that e-commerce is only a tool, just like a diet. It can claim magical properties and if rigidly adhered to the magic will work. Even the 'cabbage diet' works, but you have to be ready for it and it has to be right for you. If you are living on your own and have a poor sense of smell, it could be just what you need.

Clear definitions

The term e-commerce is so all-encompassing that it can be seen as a universal panacea. It can get you more data than you ever had access to before, and faster. It can give you real-time information, automate processes, control choice, increase choice, empower or disempower.

The danger is that organizations can lack focus on what their real purpose was in going down the e-path in the first place. Not only have many lacked focus, even when they have seen an opportunity to be taken it has been easy to be lured off the path because e-commerce and IT solutions are very flexible.

E-commerce can be defined as a set of business practices and tools that support the electronic movement of structured and unstructured business information between places and people. It does not have to involve the Internet, although it usually does. It is normally talked of in terms of linking customers and suppliers, but it can have benefits purely within a company.

Within such a broad definition a range of more specific terms have arisen. E-procurement is generally defined as the ordering of products over the Internet. E-tendering uses the Internet to present tender documents automatically and allow responses online. E-auctions are the process of running online bids for specific products.

In reality, you can tack the letter 'e' onto most purchasing processes provided that you are using a computer or the Internet. Definitions of any sort are built up through use and this market is still relatively young.

Terms can also mean different things to different people, so rather than spending too much time on them it is best simply to check what the person you are talking to thinks they mean.

Efficiency vs effectiveness

It is not merely the e-terms themselves that require definition, but also the benefits you are hoping to obtain from e-commerce. For example, the terms efficiency and effectiveness are very broad. It is possible to define them as widely overlapping – 'we are far more effective at processing orders now because auto-invoicing makes us so efficient', in other words claiming that the increased speed equals greater effectiveness.

It is also possible to give them quite separate meanings – 'We are really effective buyers: the e-auctions brought the price down 20%. We now need to look at the efficiency of the process as well.' In this instance price is being seen as 'effective' and speed as 'efficient'. This latter definition is certainly the best in terms of having targeted goals.

In considering any e-solution it is critical to have defined exactly what you want to achieve early on. You may want to get your organization fitter, for example, or thinner, or both. However, unless you have a clear goal it is likely that you will fail. Top athletes who want to get fit eat a lot. They may even put on weight, but provided it is muscle growth this is not a problem.

Product led and fear led

The e-commerce bubble was initiated by product capability and fuelled by fear. This is not necessarily a toxic combination, but both factors can have a critical downside.

Many companies want to claim that they are working with 'leading-edge technology'. On the other hand, many companies would be shy of saying that they were 'product led'. This is a dilemma. If you can see that new mobile technology could enable you to give customers faster response times, you could claim that you were being leading edge. You could also say that you were being product led: you have simply found a tool that can do something and are searching around for something to hit it with.

The difference is subtle, and significant. On the one hand, you have stumbled across 'a better mousetrap' and the world will beat a path to your door. On the other hand, you may have just invested heavily in a dealership to sell Sinclair C5s.

In the early days fear was also a considerable driver. Companies genuinely thought that new technology was going to take over the marketplace and unless they did something they would be business history. However, fear-led product development is never successful. It causes companies to be competitor focused – 'what are the competitors doing and are we moving fast enough?' – as opposed to customer focused – 'what do our customers actually want?'

These factors can combine to create muddled thinking and you need a clear form of measurement to help avoid technology that is interesting but not actually useful.

Features and benefits

There is a very effective litmus test to distinguish between these two scenarios. What is more, it explains clearly what happened with the e-commerce hype in the 1990s. The simple test is the time-honoured confusion between 'features' and 'benefits'.

Advertising has hopelessly muddled the two over many years. Take claims that 'the key benefit of Internet accounting is that you can access funds quickly' or 'one of the benefits of e-commerce is total visibility of purchased items'. These sound plausible benefits. But to be a benefit customers must have explicitly stated that they want this particular feature – only then does it become a benefit.

This was the key confusion that occurred over e-capability. Many of the claims it rightfully made were seen to be obvious benefits: speed, time saving or visibility. Nevertheless, these are only benefits if you can make use of them. It is all very well being able to place your book order online at 1 a.m. in a hotel room in Tokyo for delivery to Neasden, but if it is not in stock it can still take two weeks to arrive. In the meantime, you may have passed by the same book in several airport shops.

The allure of e-technology can tempt you beyond what your real senses tell you is a benefit. Online supermarket shopping experiences problems with what appears to be the handy feature of being able to select products easily. You simply search by product name and get a list – no longer would you have to trudge up and down aisles looking vague. In fact, most consumers cannot recognize the product descriptions they get online. 'McJohnsons Dog Crunch 1.25kg' doesn't mean much; what people know is 'the red bag with the stringy thing on and the Labrador face', which is not the sort of description that search engines find very helpful.

Perceived e-benefits

Some of the benefits claimed for companies engaging in e-commerce are:

- It will save you time.
- Ordering will be in the consumer's hands.
- Your statistics will be automatically produced.
- You will have total control.

These sorts of claims are in fact typical of the most dangerous type of feature. These are features that simply must be good for you and you can be tempted to believe in them without seeing the consequences. If this simple list is looked at in more detail, it can be seen that not all that glisters is gold in the world of e-commerce.

Time

Time saving is a key claim. The biggest danger is that it often saves a small amount of time for a lot of people. Unless the jobs that these people do are completely interchangeable, it is going to be very difficult to 'release' this time. People may be less stressed, and that is good. Or they may take a little more time to do something else more effectively, and that is good too. However, you may have savings targets based on reduced headcount, and this may not be possible.

If it does save time for one person, beware the knock-on effects on others. Consider call centres: 'In order to process your query more effectively please press 1 for . . . , 2 for . . . , 3 for . . . .' At this point most consumers are simply wishing that the bored recorded message will end ' . . . and if you want to explode the phone of the person who put this call system in, press hash . . . '

You can see the logic: a little time spent pre-qualifying customers and you can answer them more expertly. But in practice it often doesn't seem to work. Consumers feel that they are taking more time and having to do more tasks than they were before. With many e-commerce systems this sort of 'consumer tasking' can be very prevalent. Some downstream users may not only have extra tasks, these may also be taking them into new areas that stretch their personal computing skills.

Consumer control

This is particularly true of the second claimed benefit, that it will put ordering into the hands of the consumer. Online catalogue ordering is a classic example. An engineer ordering replacement parts is faced with a new process. Originally she called up her mate at Bolt-lock Systems, had a quick chat and the job was done – she may have even called him from a mobile while out on site. With the wonderful e-commerce system she has to wait until she is back in her office, negotiate passwords and portals, select drop-down lists and confirm authority levels, reason codes and use rates. It could take perhaps five times as long to do the same task. The guys in purchasing told her that it would 'transform her ordering speed' – they were certainly right.

Statistics

Automated statistics are great, but they can also generate nonsensical results. Managers at one Spanish supermarket were stunned by the number of eggs they were being asked to re-order from the e-data collected in shops. They found that local seasonal produce, which managers could buy locally and resell, didn't have a code on the new system – so they simply coded them under 'eggs' and registered the correct price. Only human intervention saved an awful lot of Spanish omelettes needing to be made.

Consumer compliance

Last but not least, anyone who claims 'you will have total buying control' is simply lying. You never can achieve this, as individuals will always have the ability to find some method to get around automated systems, even if this means buying things with their own cash and claiming them back on expenses. What is more, it is potentially dangerous to believe that you have total control, as it may stop you from seeing what you need to improve.

Real e-benefits: Efficiency

The section above is certainly not designed to be a Luddite's charter, merely a dose of reality before looking at some of the real benefits that e-commerce can bring.

Time saving

Time saving is undoubtedly a real factor and it can be a key benefit provided that the concept of 'time parcels' is understood. This was alluded to above in terms of having a time parcel that is big enough to realize a benefit.

The most usable parcel is where there are generic jobs. If you have 20 staff taking manual order sheets and entering them into a system, an online catalogue may well save a percentage of time for each of them and you would therefore be able to reduce numbers. If their roles are more expert or the operation is only part of a person's role, the percentage time savings must be significantly higher to be realized.

An example would be secretaries who also occasionally place orders. A system that makes things 20% more efficient would be good, but if it was only a task that took 20% of their time, the real saving would be only 4%. This will probably be a time parcel too small to realize.

The other management factor to remember is that no one will notice that you have saved them any time. If you are properly implementing time savings, you must have somehow reduced staff or at least redeployed resources in another way that allows you to benefit from the time saved. If you have done this effectively, everyone in the system should be back up to 100% capacity.

Even the most upbeat of software providers will admit that systems implementations rarely go according to plan. They tend to have bugs and problems in the early days that need to be fixed. If you take these two factors together you could paint a fairly dark picture. Having sold your employees the prospect of a more streamlined and efficient future, you have then put them through a period of uncertainty when initiating the change and subjected them to the extra work involved in systems migration and bug fixing. You have put them through a period of further uncertainty as you rearrange job roles to release the staff savings. And finally when it is all done they are back to working at 100% again, just like before. To cap it all, most new systems do not deliver the envisaged functionality savings.

Despite this, e-commerce does make real time savings where manual tasks can be automated and the product is one where the 'cost of acquisition' is a key target to reduce. There have been many examples of time savings where the pre-work required for tenders can be automated using e-technologies. Likewise, when the excitement of the first e-auctions has faded the repeat process can be very slick, occupying not only less physical time but also considerably less mental energy.

Managers simply need to improve their approach to such implementations. If they were going through a major redundancy process they would have a completely different approach. But efficient e-commerce is precisely that: some work that people are currently doing will become redundant. In some circumstances people will be redeployed, in others they wont. Therefore in order to make this kind of e-business work, it needs to be approached in the same way as a redeployment programme. After all, if it is not going to make any difference to how many people work in the organization or the tasks they do, why on earth are you doing it in the first place?

Consumer-based ordering

The benefits here are twofold: a simplification of the manual process, and an increased sense of responsibility for the purchase. However, there are two dark sides to these features that require careful handling.

The improvement in the manual process can be as simple as cutting out a paper process that takes time and effort. The idea of filling out an indent form and posting it off has physical elements at both ends, as the indent will need inputting into an order format. There is also the time delay as it sits in various in-trays awaiting processing. There will therefore be efficiency savings at both ends, although for consumers these will probably take time to realize, as they have to learn a new process. Even when users experience a slick online process, it is unlikely that any tangible benefits could be measured in terms of increased efficiency in their job.

The raising of responsibility is a key side benefit that is often overlooked. Under the old kind of system, you simply fill out a form saying '4 new toner pads, 15 colour cartridges and 12 reams of A4' and they all appear a few days later as if by magic. Doing this online probably shows most users for the first time the cost of each item, and perhaps other factors like delivery charges or volume/price breaks that they never knew existed.

Ultimately this has an excellent effect on consumers and often causes them to reflect on their buying habits, or indeed prompts them to think about the need for certain items. But in the short term it can cause all sorts of problems: everyone may believe, for example, that they can get a better deal at their local supermarket. They forget the cost of acquisition and often overlook the fact that they may be looking at very different quality specifications. Initially, therefore, plenty of time is taken up by purchasing professionals defending their corner on the deals they have set up, and running around trying to stop maverick buying from all sorts of different places.

There are great benefits to be achieved in this area. They can be realized much more effectively if the implementation is sold correctly.

Statistical control

The quick wins in e-commerce are almost always realized through simple leverage. Put simply, leverage is gathering your buying power into one spot and then getting a better deal because you offer more business to prospective suppliers. Once the purchases are corralled into a more focused area, you suddenly find that you were actually buying a whole load more of some things than you thought. If you are not sure of purchase volumes as you go into a more structured e-purchase system, it is worth keeping the discount or volume rebate levels flexible, so that you can return to the negotiating table with a better set of data.

One area to look out for is 'over-automation'. The downside of 'duff data in, duff data out' was illustrated above with Spanish eggs.

The other factor to watch for is reports that simply provide summary data. The increased desire for time saving has pushed people to avoid analysis work and seek an instant set of results to help with quick decision making. The challenge here is that often the pure act of manual intervention focuses the mind on trends, anomalies and exceptions that can easily be missed if you merely receive the end data.

A further aspect of this concerns the delay and costs that can be incurred as new systems are rolled out and people get a bad attack of 'report rash'. This is the highly contagious problem of everyone wanting summary reports of e-data in subtly different formats. It is always possible to do this, because 'e' can. The time and cost to get these working, however, often outweigh quite simple manual processes that could easily be done – even by senior executives.

A simple health check is to think how many times at home you have searched around for a calculator to do a sum, when in half the time you could have just sat down and worked it out on the back of an envelope.

Purchasing compliance

Many e-solutions really can increase the degree of control you have over your purchases. Most of the benefits occur through having to go through the process of getting them set up in the first place.

The set-up of e-commerce has strong analogies to the effective use of contracts. They provide a discipline to a process to ensure that all issues have been properly addressed. The simple task of agreeing specifications, prices, delivery points, access and authority levels produces one of the bread-and-butter benefits of purchasing on which many still miss out.

This set of activities can often cause a simultaneous review of processes. In many companies unnecessarily high authority levels waste time. Automated order history tracking often means that you can radically improve your authorization process. You can move from a 'papal blessing' control process (where senior managers have to sign off every nut, bolt or airfare beforehand) to a 'post hoc/ad hoc' authority trail where they do occasional checks after the event to ensure that policies are being adhered to. This cuts down on the management time involved and leaves users feeling more empowered to make sensible choices.

Once again, the dark side of control is worth understanding so that it can be appropriately tackled. There is undoubtedly an increasing business trend towards empowering those who do tasks with a greater responsibility for managing the process as well. Parts of e-commerce efficiency will help them with this, such as the ability to choose products and place orders themselves online. The counter to this is that by definition you will have limited the total range of choices to those that are within the system.

If this process is combined with supplier rationalization, which it often is, people are sure to feel some sense of disempowerment as well. They can then become astonishingly inventive in getting around the process. You can find your 'emergency ordering procedure' being invoked, invoices for 'services' that are clearly products, or bizarre lot-size repeat ordering going on to avoid higher-level authorization procedures kicking in.

How you then behave in terms of being the 'purchasing police' was discussed in Chapter 4, but once again, selling the ideas appropriately and realistically to users can avoid many of these problems occurring in the first place.

Real e-benefits: Effectiveness

While efficiency is concerned with time and process savings, effectiveness is all about saving money. There are probably only two fundamental ways in which e-commerce can deliver significant savings: first through leverage; and second through increased competition.

Leverage

The primary savings that e-commerce has claimed are probably all in the area of leverage, as we saw earlier. However, these have little to do with e-commerce, since they could be achieved by centralized purchasing the old-fashioned way. The main tool for achieving true leverage through e-commerce is the e-auction.

The original hype about e-auctions and online bidding envisaged a far more open marketplace than has actually occurred. It was thought that all sorts of companies could establish auction sites, that there would be significantly more players, and in some instances that major producers or consumers could suddenly find themselves beholden to e-trading houses for their goods and services.

One of the reasons that this never really materialized was that the customers needed to be far more diligent at understanding their own specification and volume needs. Without this information it was hard to compare quotes or to define clearly what was on offer. This stimulated some organizations to grasp, for the first time, the rather thorny issue of working out exactly how much they wanted and of what. Having done this, many found that their buying volume was far higher than they had anticipated and hence they could leverage this volume.

The second 'non-e' bonanza was to gain leverage in areas that had previously been ignored. One excellent example was a major pharmaceutical company that wanted to be a leader in e-auctions. Typical of many, it made the sensible decision to start with something quite simple, so that the risks were low. Its choice was to e-auction the purchase of 'giveaways' – baseball caps, pens, notepads and other logo-bearing promotion material – in the South American market. The results were stunning. From a total annual purchase of about $500 000, the company saved nearly $300 000.

If such a massive saving could be made so quickly, why had this area not been looked at before? There is a strong chance that even without an e-solution the company could have leveraged huge savings through a more structured approach. The reality was that this had not occurred so far, and there is no doubt that e-auctions proved to be a key enabler in making it happen.

However, leverage can sometimes bring its own problems. Large volumes are sometimes beyond the capacity or commercial desire of many suppliers. They may simply not be able to supply that volume in physical terms or may feel that such a large volume would unbalance their customer portfolio. Big is not always beautiful and can lead to a restriction on the amount of players who can compete. To combat this problem, e-commerce tools are becoming increasingly sophisticated and there are now products that can cope with different 'chunks' of business being auctioned at differing prices. This allows the higher volumes to be shown, yet more players are able to compete within the process.

Competition

There is no doubt that e-commerce – again, primarily through e-auctions – has been the key to unlocking greater competitive pressures in the marketplace. The original concept of a market rampant with aggressive e-marketplaces ripping into traditional relationships has certainly not come about.

Instead there has been a spectrum of responses. At one end, if there are only two or three suppliers capable of partaking in e-auctions it is possible to make an educated guess as to who else is bidding. This could lead to positive bid discrimination, where competitors withdraw from the auction to try to keep market prices high. With limited competition, they may be able to gain volume with another customer to compensate. In these circumstances, even the companies selling e-capability sensibly advise that it is not going to work. There has been some debate over how many competitors you need actively bidding in order to be e-effective. Theories have mooted that between seven and eight is the optimum number, but this is hard to prove. It is more likely that good old-fashioned market forces follow the normal rules: the more competition the merrier.

At the next level some suppliers simply look very hard at their own margins and make bids against their own strategic targets, without unduly focusing on the competition. These suppliers are responding to the competition of the e-process, but they never lose sight of their own bottom line, and stay customer focused rather than competitor focused.

Lastly, for those such as the 'giveaways' suppliers featured above, e-auctions have proved to work. The visibility of seeing the competition bidding on screen really affected such suppliers. In addition, the speed and ease with which the process can be repeated continues to amplify the competitive effect.

Benefits of e-exposure

Other chapters in the book have touched on the challenge for buying groups of being recognized by the rest of the business. E-commerce has made some major breakthroughs in this area.

Despite the negative potential of implementing catalogue purchasing or online ordering, it does force the buying group to engage with the organization. For many years people could have been filling out indents with no concept of what purchasing did, or even where the department was. Even if their only interaction is to complain, at least this provides a chance to gain an understanding of the needs of others within the organization and thus real mutual advantage.

E-auctions encourage interaction within a business in many ways. The pre-organization required to ensure clarity of volume and specification can be helpful and the use of new technology can be seen positively.

At a more senior level, there are several stories of the entire executive board gathering to watch the first live e-auction. As one buying manager put it: 'As they watched the bids come in there was a strange hush in the room. It was like watching the first moon landing, and was followed by a pompous speech by the chairman about how this was would "forever change our buying landscape".' No matter, purchasing was firmly on the map and seen as doing what most CEOs believe it should: bashing suppliers' prices down.

There have been some concerns that this new technology will signal the end of traditional relationships, with programmes simply automatically e-auctioning between each other. This is unlikely to occur for all but the most basic purchases. The evidence so far is that e-commerce is only fundamentally successful when strong human interaction has created the proper circumstances in which this effective and efficient tool can be used.

Concluding thoughts

E-commerce is at last starting to settle down and realize its true place in the range of tools and techniques that can be used in purchasing. There is wide consensus that it is a powerful tool that can be very effective when used in the right way.

Despite the technical and potentially impersonal nature of e-commerce, human interaction remains key to widening its use and application. Because e-commerce transactions can by their nature exclude human interaction, more care and attention needs to be paid to the relationships that surround the use of this tool.

Early 'big quick wins' are the mainstay of software consultants' sales pitches and appeal all to easily to many senior managers' short-term thinking. These will soon pass. The initial bonanza savings from the first e-auction simply cannot be repeated: excessive margins have been addressed by market forces and no longer exist to attack. This will leave more subtle savings and efficiency improvements to be worked on. While the benefits remain big, releasing them will be a tougher job.

Above all, e-commerce demands a more realistic management approach. Any change to business practices involving significant IT development will cost more than you thought, take longer than you hoped, create stress and cause short-term loss of productivity. The benefits are there and businesses should work hard to get at them – just don't fool anyone that it will be fun.

9
Outsourcing

S EVERAL YEARS AFTER IT WAS COINED, OUTSOURCING IS STILL A
buzzword. Despite occasional unwelcome headlines over jobs
being lost abroad and big outsourcing deals failing, it remains a
compelling business concept.

In the past 20 years outsourcing has become very big business.
Consultancies specializing in helping organizations outsource services
or taking over the management of services for them have mushroomed
into giant international companies. Capita and Serco, now global
operations, both grew out of the push for outsourcing in the public
sector in the 1980s. Outsourcing is the lifeblood of professional services
consultancies such as Accenture and Capgemini. IT specialists like IBM
are heavily involved in outsourcing as a major part of their business.

Yet the results of outsourcing exercises are often disappointing. A recent
survey by PA Consulting found that only a quarter of respondents were
happy with the benefits of outsourcing IT projects. Despite being
generally satisfied with suppliers' performance, nearly half said that
they would not renew the contracts, and almost three quarters reported
that outsourcing had failed to add value to their business. One in six was

planning to bring IT back in-house. Another recent survey by analysts Gartner in Europe found that half of IT outsourcing deals failed to meet expectations.

Any decision to outsource is likely to be a tricky move and is also likely to create debate and disagreement within the organization. There may be conflicting interests at play between, for example, finance and others who may be more concerned about longer-term value for money.

The purchasing professional is in the unique position of being able to assess the demands of all the parties within the organization and provide a solution in the best interests of the business as a whole. Purchasers need to be able to recommend whether to outsource and, if so, how to do it.

What is outsourcing?

Like many other business terms, the word outsourcing is open to interpretation. It could be argued that any item or service bought in by an organization from an outside source is, in effect, outsourced, and the term is sometimes used in this way.

More usually, though, the word describes an active decision to give up doing something in-house in favour of paying someone else to do it: an organization decides to hand over responsibility for a particular activity to a third party and pays an agreed price for a specified outcome.

In reality, it's an umbrella term used to describe many different kinds of relationship between two organizations in which some activity has been transferred from one to another. The nature of the relationship between the two organizations is the key to understanding how outsourcing can be effective – or not.

Make or buy

The thinking underlying the idea of outsourcing goes back to the earliest days of economic activity. Ever since the first merchant decided to pay a craftsman to fix the wheels on his cart rather than spending time doing it himself, the basic question has confronted people in business of all kinds: should you do everything yourself or get someone else to do some of it for you? The shorthand phrase underpinning discussion about outsourcing is 'make or buy'. Should you make an item or provide a service yourself using your own employees, or buy it in from someone else?

It's a very lively question in most areas of business and industry. In the construction sector, for example, building firms invariably employ subcontractors to do some of their work. Functions such as bricklaying and plumbing are, in effect, outsourced to other firms, which in turn are quite likely to employ their own subcontractors.

In a modern industrial environment, a project is likely to have several tiers of suppliers. The parent company buys goods and services from first-tier suppliers who in turn buy in from second-tier suppliers and so on. In effect, each tier, starting with the parent company, is outsourcing some of its work to the next tier.

One of the most traditional areas where the make-or-buy question is easily illustrated is manufacturing. Companies in this sector are very likely to buy in items from suppliers instead of attempting to make them for themselves. Car producers, for example, typically buy many ready-made parts from suppliers – often quite complex assemblies – to put into vehicles at the final production stage.

At its most basic level, there are some goods and services that few companies would consider carrying out themselves when there are well-established specialists in the marketplace willing to do them on their behalf. Very few businesses, for example, would think of running their own mail service. It makes perfect sense to let the Royal Mail or a commercial delivery firm do it for them. In the early days of outsourcing many organizations got rid of relatively straightforward services such as catering and cleaning.

If a company were starting from scratch and looking at every make-or-buy decision purely on merit, there would be many activities that it would immediately decide to buy in, while others would be assumed to be best done in-house. The big challenge is to decide which is which. Dividing the one from the other is at the heart of the make-or-buy question and should throw light on the debate over outsourcing.

Purchasing professionals are constantly asking themselves whether it would be better to buy in from outside or try to get something provided in-house. The outsourcing question is, therefore, central to the professional purchaser.

Close up or at arm's length

Any outsourcing decision will change the relationship between the parent organization and the function it has hived off. Indeed, the main reason for outsourcing is to give away some or all of your management responsibility for a particular activity to someone else. That saves you time and energy. However, it also means that you will have less direct control of what is done on your behalf. As with most strategic choices, there are pluses and minuses to the outsourcing option.

An in-house operation is by definition closer to the management of an enterprise than an outsourced one. It may be literally in-house, with the people carrying it out under the same roof as those who are managing it. At the very least, the people doing the activity will be employees subject to management sticks and carrots. They will be part of the company's management structure and directly answerable through their line managers to senior bosses.

An outsourced operation, on the other hand, takes away management of a function from the company on whose behalf it is being carried out. Instructions, incentives and sanctions must be filtered through a layer of management at arm's length from the parent company. This raises questions about whether the outsourced operation can fulfil the needs of the parent company in terms of cost, quality, delivery times and so on.

It may be that a third-party provider can offer an equivalent service at lower cost than that previously delivered in-house. An outside firm may even be able to offer better quality at the same or lower prices. Certainly the question of cost and quality is likely to come into the equation.

The make-or-buy continuum

Few outsourcing exercises, though, are as straightforward as the most basic definition would suggest. Most involve some level of continuing involvement by the parent company in how the outsourced activity is managed, and that is the nub of the issue. What form should the outsourcing take and, crucially, how much continuing involvement should the parent company retain over the outsourced activity?

The key variable in the different kinds of relationship under the general heading of outsourcing is the degree of management control between the two organizations. This suggests that these various kinds of relationship should be seen not as separate models but as parts of a continuum, running from one extreme where there is no management control by one organization over the other to the other extreme where it remains very powerful.

At one end of the continuum is the idea of 'back integration', which is, in a sense, the opposite of outsourcing. Instead of transferring the production of an item or provision of a service to someone else, an existing supplier is acquired by the client organization. This brings something that was once purchased from a supplier – in effect, outsourced – in-house. The reason for doing so might typically be, in the case of a manufacturing company for example, to gain greater control over prices of raw materials.

Figure 9.1 The make-or-buy continuum

Moving along the continuum in the direction of less management control lies the joint venture. This is typically an arrangement in which two organizations have agreed to exchange some management control over certain specific activities. Each organization has, in effect, outsourced something to the other.

A relationship in which two bodies in a supply chain agree to work together is what is usually known as a 'partnering' arrangement. The more dominant partner has, it could be said, outsourced some activity to the other, while maintaining a high degree of management control.

Further along the continuum is the classic outsourcing model in which one organization has relinquished management control to the other but retains ownership, in some sense, of the activity. In all likelihood it retains a right to some information about the processes involved in the activity. It will also probably retain the right to bring the activity back in-house when the contract comes to an end.

Joint ventures under the Public Finance Initiative in the public sector are an interesting and controversial variant on the outsourcing theme. In the typical PFI project (also called Public–Private Projects or PPP; there is no real difference) not only is the management of a hospital, school or other public institution outsourced to a private operator, but also its funding, building and management. The outsourcing authority typically signs a deal for up to 30 years in which it will specify a range of service levels. In return, the private company provides the entire service in line with the contract and is paid a fee, which includes a profit margin. The contractor may, as in the case of the motorway scheme in the UK Midlands, make a profit by collecting charges from users.

The argument in favour of PFI, backed by right- and left-wing governments in the last two decades, is that the private sector is providing funding and management expertise that are unavailable in the public sector. Opponents argue that it is an unethical way for private companies to make profits from public services.

At the extreme end of the make-or-buy continuum is an arrangement in which one organization pays another to produce an item or service and is unlikely to want any involvement in the activity or any form of management control: this is what would be called straightforward purchasing.

Many different kinds of relationship can be formed at any point on the continuum: it depends what is desirable and appropriate for the activity in question. Crucially, the way in which the relationship is set up depends on what is written into the contract.

Understanding these relationships is crucial for purchasing and supply management professionals. They need to understand the thinking in their organizations behind any moves towards outsourcing. They need to be able to correct any confused thinking by pointing out the potential benefits and disbenefits of any decision. They also need to make sure that the kind of relationship required has been clearly spelled out in the contract. Any terms for ending the arrangement, for example, must be thought out and included in the contract.

As we saw at the beginning of this chapter, there has been a huge amount of disappointment over outsourcing. Much of it could have been avoided if the dynamics involved had been better understood. Purchasing professionals can play a key role in this.

Why outsource?

There are many reasons for thinking that outsourcing may be a solution to a particular set of circumstances. Very often the stated reason is simple: it will cut costs. But there are many other considerations and it is as well to be aware of them to avoid unforeseen consequences.

Some reasons for outsourcing are:

- It will free up management time and resources.
- It will free up facilities, equipment and people for more important work.
- An outside supplier can provide the item/service at lower cost.
- A supplier has specialist knowledge that is unavailable in-house.
- Putting the work out to tender will test the marketplace and is likely to produce the most cost-effective outcome.
- Demand for the item/service is intermittent, making in-house investment in skills and equipment uneconomic.
- Decisions on how to maintain and improve cost-effectiveness are delegated.
- You want to shift some risk onto a third party.

- You want to make changes in personnel or working practices.

Conversely, reasons for deciding not to outsource might be:

- You will have less management control over the operation.
- It is more economical to do it in-house.
- You have spare capacity available: space, people and equipment.
- You want to develop your in-house expertise.
- If demand is intermittent, it is simpler to call on your own resources when they are needed than to contract a third party.
- It is unclear for how long a supplier may be able to fulfil your needs.
- You will lose crucial product knowledge.
- You will lose control of the supplier base and supply chain.

Most of these criteria involve weighing up countervailing pressures. And in practice, several such calculations will need to be made at the same time and considered as part of a total equation. For example, it may be that a supplier can provide an item at lower cost than its in-house equivalent, but the firm's reliability is questionable and at the same time you may have some spare capacity available in the near future. Whether outsourcing will be a sensible option overall may be a difficult decision to make.

In another situation, it may be that a company does not have the skills among its own employees to develop a particular item. The obvious solution is to find a supplier that has the expertise and can provide the item ready-made. But is that necessarily the best option? By outsourcing this activity, the company is depriving itself of the possibility of developing its own expertise in that area. It may be more economic in the long run to invest in the training and resources needed to develop the skills required.

Strategic and peripheral

One often-quoted test for deciding whether an activity is likely to be a good candidate for outsourcing is to ask whether it is central to an organization's core business. The more central it is to what your organization is all about, the less appropriate it will be for outsourcing.

According to this view, 'peripheral' activities – those that are not critical to your organization's performance – are likely to be good candidates for outsourcing. These might include catering, security or cleaning.

'Strategic' activities, on the other hand – those that are central to your business and critical to its success – should almost certainly be kept in-house. These would include management and strategic planning. Handing these functions over to an outsider would be tantamount to giving away the soul of your business.

However, it should be borne in mind that whole functions can be divided up in to their constituent parts and that some of these activities may lend themselves very well to outsourcing. Payroll management, for example, may be done just as well and at less cost by a specialist firm, while other activities within HR may be best kept in-house.

In general, again, it is largely a question of asking whether the activity is core or peripheral to your business as a whole. If it is a non-core activity and can be as reliably provided by an outsider at lower cost, it could be a very good move to outsource it.

Such formulas, however, should be treated with caution. All businesses are composed of core and non-core activities and management's job is to manage them. The cost on paper of paying someone else to manage an activity may appear attractive, but may not be truly economic in the longer term. After all, if someone else can take over the activity and make a profit on it, why give it away? With the application of a little management skill, such activities, by their nature relatively simple to operate, could be reducing costs for the parent organization.

As we have seen, the loss of management control implied by outsourcing may also not be worth suffering in exchange for some small cost savings.

Risks and benefits

Outsourcing is still in a honeymoon period. It's generally thought to be a good thing – especially, of course, by those who have made it their business. But good for whom? Any agreement to outsource must be beneficial to both parties: the one doing the outsourcing and the other taking on the activity. Alongside the potential benefits, both parties also accept an element of risk. There is always the danger of things going wrong. This means that it is crucial that the balance of benefits and risks is analysed carefully before the deal is signed.

Prices in the marketplace can go down as well as up. A company may, for example, outsource the production of an item because it can save money doing so. The supplier can provide the item at a lower cost than producing it in-house and make a profit at the same time. However, if the price of raw materials rises dramatically, the supplier risks losing money on the deal and may have to attempt to renegotiate. Conversely, if costs drop significantly, the outsourcing company may regret having outsourced in the first place.

Avid proponents of outsourcing point to the huge savings to be had from transferring operations to the East or to former eastern bloc countries. Most of the savings available come from taking advantage of the much lower labour costs in such areas.

However, a longer-term analysis may reveal that wage costs are rising in such areas: this is certainly true in some eastern European countries, especially those that have recently joined the EU. It may well be that within perhaps five years the wage rates in these regions will be approaching those of the UK. In this instance you would have borne the huge costs of the disruption, so although initially you enjoyed the benefits of lower wage costs, these would have evaporated and you would be left with the disadvantage of having set up much longer supply chains.

The logical consequence would then be to move the outsourced operation to another less-developed economy elsewhere in the world.

But the same process may occur again within a couple of years, leaving you with the prospect of moving the operation from country to country in an endless quest for lower costs. Meanwhile, moving out of your domestic marketplace might have had the knock-on effect of shrinking your home supplier base, which would make reversing the outsourcing extremely difficult. Your options would have been closed off and competitors who decided not to go for outsourcing in the first place would then be in a relatively much stronger position.

Similarly, the benefits of lower prices based on aggregated spending offered by a supplier may not last. As the supplier gains more contracts its power in the marketplace is likely to grow. It may begin to monopolize essential knowledge and skills. At the same time, its overheads will rise. What was once a good deal now becomes uneconomic, with the outsourcer locked in, not only because it has signed a contract but because it has lost the in-house skills it once had.

Intellectual property

A particular concern, especially in highly specialized areas such as IT or consultancy, is the question of how knowledge, or intellectual property, can be managed.

Very often in projects in which an outsourced supplier is working on the installation of a new IT system, for example, knowledge will be developed between the two organizations. New approaches may be the result of joint working and it will therefore be unclear who has the right to such knowledge, or data may be collected over which the supplier considers itself to have exclusive rights.

In extreme cases this can lead to a very unwelcome situation in which the outsourcing company finds that it cannot use the products of what it considers to be its own work, because the software developer holds the copyright. All such eventualities should be foreseen and taken fully into account in the contract between the two parties.

Getting it right

Outsourcing ventures, as we have said, often go badly wrong. Most are settled quietly out of court, with one side or the other writing off perhaps millions of pounds lost on the deal. Above all, it is crucial to make sure that you understand exactly what kind of relationship you are establishing with your chosen partner. You must be clear what you want them to do, while they must be clear about what you expect of them. This can best be achieved by agreeing key performance indicators.

Both sides must be clear about how the risks and benefits of the arrangement will be shared. In an IT outsourcing deal, for example, every aspect of the arrangement should be spelled out clearly in the contract. Otherwise jobs previously considered merely a part of what the in-house IT department used to do – routine downloading of data, for example – may be charged for at great expense.

Major disputes can be avoided by following some basic guidelines:

- Analyse your problem precisely.
- Define exactly why outsourcing appears to be a solution.
- Set out clearly what your role will be in the relationship.
- Establish exactly what you expect from the deal.
- Make sure you have researched the market for potential partners.
- Once you have selected a partner, establish a good working relationship between the two organizations.
- Make sure that you are fully informed how the outsourcing operation is working.

Exit strategies

If the outsourcing project is planned and managed well, it should be beneficial for both sides. But in the event that it does not work out, provision should be made for ending the contract. If the exit strategy is clear it can save a huge amount of trouble.

The exit clauses in the contract should cover the possible reasons for either side ending the contract and any penalties to be incurred. They should also make clear who is entitled to what after the break-up. In particular, any questions over the ownership of intellectual property should be anticipated. Exit clauses should cover such additional issues as whether staff from the outsourced company are free to move to the parent organization.

This is especially important where knowledge and skills have been transferred, perhaps over time. Otherwise there is a danger that the outsourcing company will find itself unable to restart the activity it has outsourced because it no longer has the expertise and is prevented from buying it back from the supplier.

Outsourcing services

The area that has created most controversy in recent years is the outsourcing of some of the more complex services that most modern enterprises need to run effectively. Ever since the cost-cutting 1990s, the whole gamut of services have come under the outsourcing microscope. Some, such as catering and cleaning, are relatively straightforward because the measurable outcomes required by the outsourcing company are fairly simple. More complicated functions such as financial services, customer services and HR have also been targeted. Outsourced call centres, especially in financial services, have attracted a huge amount of publicity.

To a greater or lesser extent, all these services lend themselves to being provided by an outside third party. Catering, for example, is not something in which most companies are likely to have any expertise, so it makes little sense to develop and maintain it in-house. It is far more cost-effective to pay someone else to run your canteen and provide refreshments for your meeting rooms. The obvious exception would be companies whose main activity is catering.

More complex services present more difficult challenges. It is one thing to pay an agency to provide your receptionists and security staff, but quite another to hand over responsibility for your HR function to an outside firm.

The key question is the basis on which such decisions should be made. That means analysing the nature of the relationship that you envisage with your outsourced provider.

Outsourcing purchasing

Ultimately, purchasing professionals may have to ask themselves whether their own function should continue to be in-house or whether it too should be outsourced. Several companies have attempted this, with mixed results, but there is no reason in principle why it should not be successful. Purchasers may like to question if they see their work as a core activity within their organization and whether this is the key factor.

Like any other area of activity, the essential safeguards are to make sure that the reasons for considering the outsourcing of purchasing are clear and that, if it goes ahead, the contract is set up effectively with all the necessary targets and penalties to ensure the desired outcomes.

As with any other function, certain activities within purchasing may make good candidates for being hived off. The transactional side of the function, for example, may lend itself to being run more efficiently by an outside provider. Or particular categories may be better purchased by a specialist outsider. In many ways purchasing outsourcing can work very well because the outsourcing provider can sign up to specific cost-saving targets and the pricing can be linked to these, guaranteeing a win–win outcome.

IT

IT is one of the biggest areas in which outsourcing now plays a major role. The ways in which companies arrange their IT provision with third-party suppliers illustrate the range of options available.

A company might, for example, enter an agreement to pay for the installation of its IT systems and run the operation using its own in-house employees. Another firm may decide that it does not have the expertise in-house to handle day-to-day enquiries about operating the systems, so it outsources the help-desk operation to the software provider. Another organization may be happy to relinquish direct control of its systems and is therefore happy to pay the IT services provider to look after them entirely on its behalf.

Call centres

The controversy over the outsourcing of call centres makes them worth looking at as an example of the arguments for and against such moves.

The arrival of computerized telephony in the late 1980s made it possible to route calls automatically to operatives as soon as their lines became free in a continuous stream, thus cutting out wasted time. The call centre, in which sometimes large numbers of staff are engaged solely in dealing with enquiries, made good economic sense.

In many ways call centres were an ideal candidate for outsourcing. Telephone enquiries were usually routine and could be handled effectively by staff with little direct connection to the parent company. Minimal training was required.

The big incentive, though, was cost. With wages in India and other countries a fraction of those in the UK, coupled with cheap and efficient international telecommunications, the arguments in favour of outsourcing call centres to low-cost countries in the developing world were powerful.

However, there were minuses as well as pluses and we are witnessing something of a reversal in the trend. In 2004 the Alliance and Leicester bank and Northern Rock building society both decided not to outsource their call centres but to build up these services in the UK instead.

The question of cost and quality at the heart of all purchasing decisions is once again raising itself. Financial services companies have saved a great deal of money by outsourcing their call centres, but at a potential cost. Apart from the risk of bad publicity over the export of jobs abroad, it has become apparent that an operative in another country may be unable to offer the same level of service to customers compared to that provided by an employee based in the company's own premises in the UK.

Concluding thoughts

There is more to outsourcing than is often realized. It is not a simple cost-cutting technique and can be far more difficult to manage than an in-house operation.

Outsourcing is therefore not a black-and-white decision. It is part of a continuum including many other forms of contractual arrangement between organizations. While an outsourced operation is normally considered to be one in which a large measure of control over the activity concerned has been delegated to another organization, there are many variations on this kind of relationship.

There are huge risks associated with outsourcing that must be carefully analysed in advance of making any such move. The disastrous results of badly researched outsourcing projects are legion.

Purchasing professionals have an extremely important role to play in advising on the merits or otherwise of outsourcing projects and need to be aware of their intricacies.

10
Globalization

THE CONCEPT OF GOING GLOBAL CAN INVOKE A WIDE RANGE OF reactions, and all for the same reasons. At one end of the scale you have howls of protest at the evils of creating uniformity, of crushing individualism and of putting finance first. At the other end of the spectrum – perhaps more in the boardroom – you have howls of protest against the evils of specification diversity, lack of corporate identity and the loss of financial clout.

Despite these high emotions, the concept of globalization is still not particularly clear. The word is a nominalization – a verb turned into a noun. Anyone who tries to define such a concept always has a real challenge. For example, virtually every business in the world believes that it needs 'better communication', but very few of them can define what this means. The same is true for globalization. Many businesses believe that they must go down that route in order to survive in today's changing climate, although exactly what 'going global' means will be very diverse.

This chapter will look at the benefits and pitfalls of going global, how best to manage the situation and where the future for this type of activity will lie.

The path to globalization

Even without taking a cynical view of life, there is no doubt that in the commercial world the concept of globalization is an attractive one. If you type the phrase 'global buyer' into any 'job search' database engine, you will get a lot of hits. There is clearly something in adding it to the job title (or indeed, retrospectively to your CV) that most people believe will add to its attractiveness. You even find it attached to quite junior roles – 'global sourcing expeditor' sounds quite grand, but with a salary of '£14 500–16 500' it is more likely that this is what used to be called a shipping clerk.

A second factor that encourages the development of the concept is the well-known consultancy challenge of getting people to look at any given subject in both more depth and more breadth. Advice to many boards started with the concept of moving from simple buying to the greater depth of supply chains, and it has now attained breadth by talk of global supply chains.

The development of globalization and that of partnerships have some common attributes that provide very useful learning. They are both 'grand ideas' – it seems that not only are there some obvious benefits to be had, but also they have a very 'strategic' feel about them. You are never going to be sacked from the board for saying: 'What we need is expanded global reach through a series of integrated networking partnerships.'

Both of these concepts do have real potential, but it can only be realized if they are pursued with a great deal of discrimination. A key metric to test them against is: 'Is this a means to an end or the end of a means?'

This is where so many global (and partnership) initiatives have failed. If you take the definition of global purchasing as having established a network of real buying options around the world, that is going to take time. Simply having a global intent and retro-fitting a few pieces of international purchasing into it does not make for a working strategy.

Global vs international

As with many other areas of purchasing, the relatively young nature of the profession means that agreed definitions are still quite varied. Defining terms can be the rather self-indulgent domain of consultants and academics. It can also be useful at least to understand the differences between these ideas, especially if you are setting off down the path of going global. Terms such as 'international' and 'global' are often interchanged. The differences may be subtle, but they can be important. The comparison in Table 10.1 helps illustrate this.

Many companies that claim to operate global buying do so because they have one central buying point and buy from all over the world. However, this is not global buying, simply international sourcing. The concept of globalization means having a real understanding of and presence in a range of markets. It is not enough simply to be buying from them. This local knowledge is the main factor that allows the real benefits of global

Table 10.1

International	Global
• Core buying group at one location	• A clear organization with local empowered buyers
• Limited manufacturing locations	• Many manufacturing locations
• Specifications adapted to meet international supplier capability	• Suppliers adapt production to meet one central specification
• Currency variations managed through hedging	• Currency variations balanced through alternative supplies
• New buying needs negotiated to improve leverage	• New buying needs fit into existing framework agreements

purchasing: it provides the knowledge and flexibility that can allow an agreed framework agreement to be achieved.

However, the relationships and framework for global purchasing require heavy up-front investment. This is why it is important to distinguish between a desire to buy internationally – which may solve a tactical problem – and the desire to be truly global. The latter should only be undertaken when the company has the capacity in almost every sector – that is, production, locations, people and deep pockets – to make it viable.

The benefits of going global

Even if going global did start as a boardroom fashion statement, the reality is that there are some benefits that can be realized beyond having a fancy title on your business card and hoping that will work its way back into a higher salary.

In looking at any business concept a framework model can be useful. Marketing has the famous 'Four Ps' (Price, Product, Place and Promotion). The concept of global buying can be looked at in terms of its 'Four Ls': Level playing field, Leverage, Learning and Logistics.

Level playing field

The benefits here lie in two main areas. First is the astonishingly simple concept of being supplied with the same thing at the same price from the same supplier. Secondly, creating uniformity in purchases allows you to simplify processes and unlock the real benefits of leverage.

The first of these benefits may appear to be common sense of the highest order. However, there continue to be large opportunities from this area. Even such apparently minor issues as a different pricing currency can create a fog to obscure the benefits. It is of course very simple to calculate that at today's exchange rate your glass supplier is cheating you by charging more in Bremen than Birmingham. The muddle starts as exchange rates move – three months later and the same supplier is cheating you the other way around. Your company then decides to move its reporting currency to euros and leaves you really scratching your head as to which price to argue for.

Inter-company statistics are notorious for inconsistency, either in reporting units or simply a lack of data. Taking a global approach can start to iron out these issues and can give buyers real data to negotiate with. There is a tendency among buyers to believe that the selling company is basking in a profiteering bonanza of differential pricing. The reality tends to be that the selling organization has exactly the same problems as the buyer and it is far more a case of 'cock-up' than 'conspiracy theory'. As simple as this concept sounds, it contains a real rough oyster that needs hard work to prize it open to find a pearl. The heart of this benefit lies in basic systems and accounts and is about detail and determination – all rather unsexy stuff.

The second part of this benefit is in getting a uniform specification. One purchasing director, from a Finnish paper company, made a challenging statement that goes to the heart of this issue: 'You are only really a global purchaser when you have a single specification and it is written in English.'

This is certainly the sort of statement that can draw all kinds of comments – not least about xenophobia. The reality is that if you do have to choose a single business language, English is going to be it. If the specification is in English that is also an indication of the degree of acceptance of a uniform approach. The concept of uniform culture will be tackled later in this chapter, but the harsh reality is that if your excuse for translating specifications into another language is to allow for 'cultural sensitivity', you have clearly not established a common culture. It is also worth remembering that it was a Finn who made the remark in the first place.

The key issue is that if you do have a single specification, it does mean that all your plants are running the same process for this product – or at least one that can cope with uniformity. Even minor changes in operation and information flow can have major impacts, often known as the 'Forrester effect' or 'bullwhip effect'. Although the theory that produced this term (expounded by MIT's Jay Forrester in *Industrial Dynamics*) dealt with product demand variations, the same is also true of the knock-on effects of other kinds of diversity, such as different specifications for raw materials.

Leverage

Perhaps the most popular benefit (in both spread and value) of globalization comes from leverage. In its simplest form in this context, this is the ability to aggregate a diverse set of purchases from around the world into a single unit that can appear more attractive to a supplier. There are also subtler definitions of leverage benefits that can include the comparison of quality, as well as the comparison of cost base.

'Stack 'em high and sell 'em cheap' is a well-known phrase. Everyone understands its implicit assumption that if you have lots of something, you can probably sell it cheaply because you must have bought it cheaply. This lies behind the widely held business belief that you will get a better deal if you aggregate your spending.

Purchasing managers who have been through the experience of working this theory on a global scale have found it to be a mixed blessing, and even suppliers are starting to question their hunger for entering such marketplaces. First, there are real benefits. Even if sellers may not be that attracted to higher sales (perhaps due to production bottlenecks), they may well be forced down that route for fear of losing those parts of the deal that they already serve. The combination of greater organization on a global scale and the appropriate use of tools such as e-auctions will continue to generate millions in savings. The downsides to be aware of, however, are that sometimes large buying volumes can restrict the choice of supplier. Not only that, but you will also be left with the biggest players in the supply market – and if they have been reading the right marketing books, they should be price leaders rather than price followers.

In addition, some suppliers have realized that they get lured into a destructive cycle. Companies globalize purchasing and increase their demand, so suppliers respond with aggressive bidding. The loser, afraid of being eclipsed, may well take an even more aggressive stance at the next opportunity. The winner – now much closer to full production – may back off. One leading European metal drum manufacturer bemoaned the fact that after three years of this behaviour he believed all the suppliers had exactly the same market share as before, only all the prices were lower. This can be great for buyers in the short term, but it can cause market rationalization; prices can then climb back strongly and there is less competition to keep them in check.

The second, more subtle area for leverage is the use of lower-priced markets to 'lever down' the price of an existing supplier. Globalization plays a key role in this, where developing economies with both exchange-rate and cost-of-living advantages can be brought into more established marketplaces. East European, Russian, Far Eastern and Asian markets have all had their role to play in this area. The trend of moving call centres to eastern Europe or India is a good example of this, discussed in the previous chapter. The strategic (and sometimes very sensitive) nature of the decision often means that it is more often taken in the boardroom than the buyer's office, but the process is one of global leverage. The product in this case is people, and the global market allows for a higher-spec individual to be supplied at a lower price.

The challenge of using leverage through price comparison lies in being confident that all the factors of total cost have been considered, not merely the price. Sourcing from a distant market will involve the obvious additional costs of freight and insurance. There have been examples of people forgetting other costs such as customs duties, although the real hidden costs can be in quality audits, dispute resolution or the inherent risks of a more vulnerable supply chain.

Learning

The concept of learning through a more global approach has depths and benefits at a variety of levels.

At its simplest level, new sources and/or different levels of quality can be found that could be more suitable. This might mean an even higher or purer specification. There is the famous story of the first time a new Japanese supplier was asked to supply product to 98% accuracy. As it only shipped product to 100% accuracy it was a little perplexed, eventually shipping 98% of the consignment that was accurate and deliberately making and separately packing the other 2% 'off spec' in order to meet the order's requirements.

On the other hand, lower-quality – or, to be more precise, 'fit for purpose' – products are often the ones that can be found in alternative markets, and these can generate significant savings.

The next level up is to learn not only about new suppliers, but also about their cost bases and processes. These are most likely to be unique to each supplier, even when they are apparently operating a similar process. You can be almost certain that local conditions and management have adapted or improved things in specific ways. They may on the surface be operating the same 'Brownings extraction process and centrifugal separation', yet within the detail could be significant changes that can yield comparative benefits. As a buyer you are in a unique position to understand these, as the supplier is hardly like to explain it in too much detail to its competitors.

For those who are experienced in working for larger companies, it will come as no surprise that among the hardest kind of learning to release is that of your fellow company workers. In some well-entrenched 'local' markets, buyers may even be more inclined to share information with their suppliers than they would with head office. It is true that they work for the same company, yet they may see very little benefit in this type of sharing. Global organizational models usually follow long after the concept of sharing globally has been announced. There is often very little line management authority to support sharing behaviour, and for some country-based organizations such sharing may only appear as a net cost. If regions keep being called to attend new group conferences, they bear all of the travel and time costs locally, but many of the benefits they bring are given to others to reap profits outside of their domain. If the job is approached with a keen eye for the personal selling of benefits and appreciation of the other buyers' point of view, as well as some form of recognition for useful behaviour, it will be a success. This is not exactly the most stunningly original formula for a good result, but what is most stunning is how often it is overlooked.

The key to real success in this area is to reverse the obvious logic of the global idea. Most people still see learning as a useful side benefit to the process of going global. Instead of saying 'we are going global so let's do that and see what we learn', it can be approached by saying 'we need to learn more widely so let's go and seek that in a more global context'. This may sound like a syntactical shift, yet it can change the way buyers look at opportunities as they arise.

Logistics

Globalization and logistics form a two-edged sword. On the one hand, you can have stretched supply lines and untested relationships that can increase the vulnerability of your supply chain. On the other hand, the fresh relationships can break old market cartels, and in many instances a new global source can offer shorter shipping times and increased security through wider stock points.

Logistical benefits were probably among the first that caused alternative supplies to be found, when a range of intrepid buyers sought alternative supplies from further away. Such a move was certainly more tactical than strategic. It was driven more by an existing problem than a desire to transform the supply chain into one that would be of benefit in the longer term. Some initiatives were even started by the logistics companies themselves, with empty ships or trucks searching for 'back-haul' opportunities, therefore starting new supply routes.

Whatever the starting point, the two key logistical benefits lie in the classic areas of costs and security. The cost element can be as simple as shortening distances. When South Africa emerged from its general level of isolation in the 1990s it provided an excellent new source for many products. Even without its hunger to get into world markets, it made much more sense to ship products from South Africa to the Far East than from Europe.

The concept of security benefits can be a little more complex. Whenever alternative suppliers are being sought, there is by definition the risk of a new relationship. While this may be a chance to broaden the choice of suppliers, it is not always easy to judge the long-term commitment of new players. They will all talk a good partnership story, yet until the product has flowed for a time it is hard to tell what issues arise. Even if existing specifications can be met, there have been numerous examples where an alternative supply is found to have a different manufacturing impact through trace elements that were not originally specified. There will also be more time consumed in testing products, quality assurance work and logistics coordination. Simple challenges like time differences and language barriers increase workloads, and often in areas outside of purchasing. The benefits will need to be sold effectively to those implementing such changes if they are to be embedded successfully.

Where these benefits may arise

The benefits from each 'L' will always depend on individual circumstances. Sometimes simply levelling price differentials can make massive differences. In other situations you can discover that there are no differentials on which you can make savings. As a broad rule, however, there will be certain situations where one of the areas is more likely to yield benefits, and these can be mapped against the classic comparison of market forces vs buying power (Figure 10.1).

Where the risk and cost are low, maximizing the logistical benefits is important for tactical purchases, where the cost of acquiring the goods needs to be kept down. More critical purchases are where establishing a

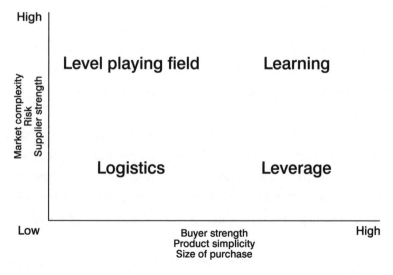

Figure 10.1

clear level playing field is important. Although buying size may be quite low, these are important products and benefits will flow through a clear understanding of how these purchases are valued across any group.

The strategic sector is an excellent area in which to gain learning from other markets. Here there will be mutual understanding of the importance of the purchase both within the buying side and between the buyer and seller – and true learning is what a partnership is all about. The leverage sector probably speaks for itself.

How to realize these benefits

The benefits of working on a global scale require a successful organizational structure to allow them to be realized. The hope that everyone in the group is pulling together to the same ends is often a forlorn one. Even if your purchasing group is united under a common management structure throughout the organization, you still have a variety of options on how you can set out your stall. Do you choose to centralize expertise in one area, or should you run satellite operations in each location?

There are some simple and logical factors that can help with this decision. There is also a range of illogical, personal and power-political reasons for organizing global purchasing in a certain way (Figure 10.2). These factors often get in the way of the underlying issues that need to be addressed as the department seeks a wider sphere of coordinated effort.

These two axes can provide a good source of reference for making choices. However, like all simple headlines they do carry some health

Figure 10.2

warnings that require some understanding. Broadly speaking, as you move to the top right-hand side of the matrix, a more centralized approach is likely to prove successful. It may be that with big and uniform purchases you have to go for a more forceful approach if your culture is not yet aligned. Certainly, if you are at the bottom left corner then a centralized approach is going to be doomed and a local solution will be best. The 'beware' box is the one where groups have a willingness to cooperate, yet lack any serious issues on which to work. This can be a very time- and resource-consuming box, good for picking up air miles, but not an area that is going to yield many other benefits.

The other risk area is where you become fooled by your own company brochure and believe that you have a common culture already. It may well be that you have achieved true global harmony of processes. This may also have been written for the chairman by a PR firm which wouldn't know one end of a process from the other. In other words, you need to be very frank about whether you do have a common culture, or whether it is still at the aspirational stage. Have you really got the Basingstoke depot working to the same plan yet, or were you hoping that it will come round in time?

Until a common culture is starting to be felt, the most valuable benefits will not be realized. Once there are true desires to achieve a common culture, the biggest benefits can be unearthed through buying streams.

Buying streams

The use of buying streams works well in the situation where you do have a more common culture (or the basis to build one) and there is a decent size of benefit to be worked on. Because these streams can be so successful, it is worth exploring them in more detail.

Buying streams are where you have brought together a range of interested parties to develop a more unified approach. The rules for success are:

- No more than six people on the team.
- Production/technical representation.
- Buyers from at least two locations.
- Biggest user site represented.
- Most awkward user represented.

The streams need to balance representation with the ability to make decisions. If users are well represented, this gives a strong chance of streams both challenging and delivering the art of the possible. They can also partake in genuine group negotiations and, with careful orchestration, can be enormously effective. The combination of different styles, viewpoints and passions can be a potent force. Suppliers have a tendency to respond by concentrating their knowledge in one more senior sales person, and this can be to their detriment.

The stream must also have a finite life, and it is important that there are no line management relationships between the members of the stream. This is why it should be called a stream, not a team. The goal for the business is uniformity of both product and culture. These are always only truly embedded through cooperative attitudes at a working level. The stream is a working example of what is required. Its members should come together, gain understanding and respect for a more common goal, and for the local needs to deliver it. Once the project has been delivered, they can disband, return to their origins, and will often be the most powerful ambassadors for cultural change within the group.

The one downside of this type of organization is that it is resource hungry. It not only takes time to set up, but the running costs are high. People need to meet face to face; they need to see each other's operations to truly understand the local factors that could make a central deal less workable. In addition they need to meet a lot, particularly in the early phases where mutual understanding and the respect for diversity are critical. Provided that big expenditure is at stake the investment is worth making, as it will be paid back through the key benefit areas of learning and leverage.

What next after globalization?

In 2003 the global food and drinks business Diageo announced a reshaping of its global purchasing initiative. It had been a pioneer in this area, and perhaps like many pioneers found that once early benefits had been realized the ongoing investment was going to be harder to justify.

There is a modern business mantra that unless you continue to grow your global reach you will be left on the sidelines and others will dominate the market. This may be true for selling products, but it may not be the case for purchasing products. Even with a global brand, it could be possible to support it through local purchasing.

There is a growing body of organizational thinking that groups have a critical size, beyond which the benefits of bulk are outweighed by the problems of communication and commitment. Any organization needs to pay attention to the way it coordinates and communicates, and when you are doing this on a global scale it is increasingly difficult to maintain. Modern communication methods flatter to deceive. The idea that the CEO or head of purchasing can speak on a daily basis to everyone in the organization via online video streaming is a classic such problem. This is not communication; at best it is information delivery and at worst it is dictation.

In addition to this, globalization has a bad name generally. It can be characterized as an over-dominant force, a manipulator of markets, a destroyer of local culture. Although these are strong words, they do have some element of truth for buying. The purpose of real global buying *is* to be a dominant market force, to manage markets and to create uniformity. Some companies may feel that being seen this way is not worth the publicity it could generate and the possible backlash by either consumers or overstretched suppliers.

It is likely that truly global activities will be few and far between. Certain specific products, in certain companies, in certain markets will stand the test of time. For the majority global purchasing will be a project, an initiative. This is not bad; it is simply the likely outcome. The skill will lie in managing sufficient commitment to the necessary up-front resource, with the appropriate check on reality to deliver benefits and not soundbites.

Concluding thoughts

Going global is not the Holy Grail to be sought at great cost and by all worthy folk. Nevertheless, it has some great benefits that can be leveraged for certain types of purchasing categories.

The leverage that you can gain is usually one-off. While the numbers can be big, the long-term benefits of learning will always be greater. Measuring these is a challenge and far-sighted management will be needed to support the process.

The simplest of processes to gain common specifications, prices or logistical savings are sometimes passed over as the early quick wins of a project. These should not be underestimated: they are not only a win for now, but they have a lasting legacy in terms of a common platform to enable future development.

In many ways globalization is not such a grand idea. Its benefits are reached through simple good practice, and the focus needs to be on this rather than the boardroom concept of a global presence.

11
Ethics

THE CONCEPT OF WHAT IS ETHICAL CAN VARY FROM organization to organization and culture to culture, and is often very difficult to decide. Consider the following scenarios.

Nothing but the truth

You are a senior purchaser at a major multinational. You strike a deal with a small local firm to supply a large volume of goods for a long period of time. You know that the supplier will have to invest in equipment and take on more staff to fulfil the order. However, you also know that there has been discussion at board level in your own company about closing down the division dealing with this particular line. Are you under any obligation to tell your supplier that there is a good chance of the order being cancelled halfway through?

A bribe by any other name

You are dealing with a supplier abroad who insists that to close the deal you must pay a third party who will take a 'facilitation fee'. You strongly suspect that this is a way of diverting part of the payment to someone's private bank account – a bribe. If you refuse, you will lose the deal. Do you go along with it?

Sheer exploitation

You discover that your company is sourcing a particular product from a developing country where children are being forced to work long hours and paid next to nothing. After visiting the site, you realize that stopping the use of this supplier will mean many families losing their only source of income. Should you insist on sacking the supplier?

It's in the air

Like many of your peers, you accept frequent-flyer miles direct from airlines whenever you book a business trip. You use them to help fund your family's leisure travel. Your employer has tried unsuccessfully to stop the practice and plough the benefits back into company funds. You and your colleagues know that it is in effect an inducement from the airlines to do business with them, and you have sometimes chosen a flight because the frequent-flyer allowance is generous, even though it's not the best value available. Is this an acceptable perk for a hardworking executive or, in effect, a bribe from the airline companies?

French leave

A supplier has organized a conference to which you have been invited. It's in the South of France, and you have been offered not only free travel and accommodation at a top hotel for the duration of the conference, but also a couple of extra days at the end with a free wine-tasting tour and other goodies thrown in. You can take annual leave for the extra days, but with negotiations due to take place on a major deal, you suspect that the free trip is meant to sweeten you up. Is there any harm in accepting the offer?

Mixing business with pleasure

As head of your department, you look after your own diary and spend a lot of time out of the office. Most of it is on official business, but you sometimes take an afternoon or a whole day off to play golf with friends and colleagues from other companies. You talk shop some of the time, but mainly it's simply a chance to escape the pressures of work and relax. Is this time well spent developing contacts and exploring new ideas, or an abuse of your responsible position?

Taking responsibility

These scenarios are fairly typical of the kinds of challenges facing purchasing professionals from time to time. They all raise important ethical issues. Some are very tricky. What would you do faced by each of these situations?

There are not necessarily any correct answers. Much depends on your judgement. But the important point is that you consider the rights and wrongs of the situation and make a decision. That is what ethics is all about.

As philosophers point out, we are all making ethical decisions much of the time, not merely at work but in our private lives too. Questions such as 'Should I do this?' and 'Would it be right to say that?' are fundamental to our experience as human beings. These are questions involving ethical concepts.

Ethics in purchasing

There are many ways in which ethics come into play for a professional purchaser. At the most everyday level, there are questions of the kind we all come up against at work, as in the 'French leave' scenario above. Then there are bigger questions about relating to suppliers, like the 'nothing but the truth' story above. And finally there are significant issues to do with how purchasing policies can have consequences for those affected by them, like the 'sheer exploitation' story.

Everyone faces such questions, but for purchasing professionals they are often far more acute than for those in other functions. As the people responsible for spending the company's money and choosing between suppliers, purchasers are in a particularly powerful position. But this also makes them extremely vulnerable. It's not generally thought such a big deal if a sales person, for example, spends rather generously on a lunch for a potential customer. Indeed, sales people are often given an entertainment budget specifically to spend on wooing customers into signing deals. Purchasing people, on the other hand, must be seen to be above any suspicion of being swayed by such considerations.

This suggests a double standard: companies encourage their sales people to spend money on customers, but alarm bells will ring if a purchaser benefits from exactly the same kind of generosity from a supplier. Nevertheless, it's a double standard that makes perfect sense. Because of their powerful position purchasers must be seen to be ethical, whatever goes on in the rest of the organization.

Projecting an ethical image

Ethics, however, is not only about establishing a series of rules about what you should not do. It is also about what it is desirable to do. Ethical behaviour is as much about 'thou shalt' as 'thou shalt not'.

There are many instances in recent years of companies falling foul of public opinion when it has been discovered that their suppliers were, for example, exploiting children in developing countries, ignoring basic health and safety protection or denying workers basic rights. Major corporations such as Nike, Starbucks and McDonald's, for example, have all faced high-profile accusations of operating unethical supply policies.

But the commercial world is also full of examples of companies doing good. From small firms sponsoring local events to multinationals taking a stand on exploitation in developing countries, commerce can be a force for social progress. Ethical considerations are now a priority on the financial services scene, for instance. In pure business terms, doing the right thing can add value to your organization by helping project a positive image, just as doing the wrong thing can destroy value.

'Corporate social responsibility' (CSR), the catch-all phrase used to encompass the ways in which organizations can avoid making ethical mistakes and promote good policy, is a key consideration in all sectors. This is partly because consumers are becoming more and more aware of how the goods and services they buy are produced. They are less willing to support those organizations they judge to be acting in an unethical or irresponsible way.

CSR includes the question of how organizations treat the environment. A growing body of public opinion demands that companies actively promote policies to lessen the impact of their activities on the earth's natural resources. Many organizations make environmental concerns a priority. Some, the do-it-yourself chain B&Q for example, have put caring for the environment in their supply chains at the heart of their business.

Right and wrong

Discussions of ethics can easily be scuppered by confusion over terms. But most attempts at basic definitions fail to throw any light on the concepts involved.

Ethics, one such definition claims, is 'concerned with the moral principles and values which govern our beliefs, actions and decisions'. But what are moral principles and values? What does moral mean? Does it mean the same as ethical? How can you tell when something is moral and when it is not? You're back where you started, asking what 'ethics' means. This is because the concept of 'good' is irreducible. It cannot be defined except in terms of itself.

It would be well-nigh impossible to explain the difference between right and wrong to someone who didn't seem to understand. Luckily for busy working people, though, most of us know right from wrong without having to think about it too much. Most people have been brought up with these concepts and they have become almost instinctive.

However, that doesn't mean that there's no point in discussing ethical issues. Every business faces ethical challenges and it's up to everyone involved, at all levels, to take part in the debate about how the company and other organizations should behave.

Purchasing professionals can play a key role in this because, as we have seen, they have a unique role as the people responsible for awarding contracts to suppliers. Purchasers who subscribe to ethical values are in a strong position to help set the tone of an organization, whether it is a company, a voluntary organization or a public-sector body such as a local authority. Indeed, because of their position at the cutting edge of an organization, they have a special responsibility to help set and maintain ethical standards.

The moral dilemma

The real questions we all face are about how we apply ethical values in everyday life – about how to decide in specific situations what is right and wrong. It's not always easy, as we've seen. These questions often take the form of a moral dilemma, where you have to balance opposing arguments and, sometimes, decide on the one that appears to be the 'lesser evil'.

In these situations, it is especially important to think clearly about what is involved. It may be necessary to make an awkward decision with which you are not totally happy. But real life presents such dilemmas from time to time and you have to deal with them. Crucially, though, you must be clear about what is involved and not try to justify your decision dishonestly.

Wrong can't be right

Is it ever acceptable to justify doing something that you know is wrong by arguing that it is in fact not really wrong at all?

Everyone knows, for example, that copyright should be protected because royalties from books, recordings and so on pay the wages of those who produce and sell them. So most people would not buy counterfeit CDs from a dodgy stall at a car boot sale. But what if someone at work offers to burn a copy of a CD that you like, but are unlikely to buy?

The obvious, off-the-top-of-your-head answer is that it's OK because it's not really going to make any difference to anyone. However, that argument taken to its logical conclusion means that ethical considerations are based only on the size of the activity concerned: if it's OK to accept one illegally copied CD, it must be OK to buy counterfeit CDs by the hundred and, indeed, to make money out of producing them.

The truth is simple: dealing with counterfeit material is wrong, no matter how big or small the volumes may be. For a professional purchaser this is especially relevant, because of all the inherent dangers in buying fake goods. Counterfeit items have been identified as the cause of disasters all over the world from plane crashes to famine.

The same applies in other situations. Defrauding your employer to the tune of thousands of pounds is obviously a bad thing to do. But what about exaggerating your expenses? The same logic applies: size makes no difference. If it's wrong, it can't be right.

The eleventh commandment

Another everyday justification for unethical behaviour says, essentially, it's all right if you can get away with it. It may be wrong to accept a small inducement, but it somehow becomes acceptable if you can obey the eleventh commandment: 'thou shalt not get caught'.

The risk of getting caught is undoubtedly a serious consideration. You could be faced with a serious reprimand, affecting your relations with colleagues and, at least temporarily, holding up your career, or you could get the sack. You could even end up facing a prison sentence.

The eleventh commandment argument is a purely utilitarian view that taken to its logical conclusion conjures up a world with no ethical standards, where survival of the fittest rules and only number one matters.

Reality check

Having said all that, it does appear sensible to keep a sense of proportion. Accepting a bribe to award a contract is indefensible, but it seems churlish to say that no purchaser should ever accept anything from a supplier. It's important to make sure that any such gifts do not affect the purchaser's judgement when making decisions about awarding contracts and dealing with suppliers. This, however, is very difficult to judge when looking at yourself.

That is why the involvement of others is crucial. It's not just a question of doing the right thing but of being *seen* to do the right thing. Like everyone else, purchasing professionals must try to appear to their colleagues and the world outside as honest and straightforward in their dealings.

To be seen otherwise is negative, however minor it may seem. It applies not only to business dealings. Take a purchasing professional who announced that he was going to go on a sponsored marathon and collected sponsorship from his colleagues. The race was duly held and the purchaser collected the money. It was some time after the event when one of the donors heard that the purchaser had not, in fact, finished the race. Challenged on this, he replied, 'Oh well, it was for a good cause, and anyway you should have checked whether I finished or not.'

It could be argued this was an insignificant 'white lie'. But it called the purchaser's honesty into question, and that is likely to remain a stain – albeit a small one – on his reputation for some time to come. On balance, it's best to avoid this kind of thing.

It's a gift

One of the most controversial issues among purchasing professionals in recent years has been the question of whether you should accept gifts from suppliers. Some take the view that all gifts are unacceptable and should be refused or returned to the sender. Such gifts are meant to influence the purchaser's judgement when deciding who to award contracts to, and should be rejected if only simply to be on the safe side. You must be seen to be totally unbribable.

Others take a more relaxed view. As long as all gifts are out in the open and are not allowed to cloud your judgement, there is no harm in accepting them on a modest scale. If they can be used in the office as raffle prizes or rewards for hard-working staff, or given to charity, then there is little question of individual gain.

The issue becomes much more complicated when considering business dealings with suppliers in which they are asked to contribute to the purchaser's organization in some way by, for example, agreeing to sponsor an activity by means of a cash donation. This becomes an issue about purchasers using undue pressure on suppliers, which, almost by definition, is unethical. The difficult question to answer is when a reasonable suggestion that sponsorship might be beneficial to both parties becomes a threat on which continuation of the contract depends. Where that line is drawn must in the end depend on the purchaser's judgement.

However, there are many different, often conflicting points of view, and the question of who is right is often impossible to pin down. It is in the nature of ethics that personal judgement sometimes has to be the arbiter of what is right and wrong. Old-fashioned conscience – that nagging, tell-tale feeling that something isn't quite right – still has a major role to play.

Ethical supply chains

A group of senior government procurement directors were discussing some of the points made at a seminar run by a leading university. Among other topics, the speaker touched on the need for government purchasing policy to help tackle problems such as poverty in the developing world.

A fierce debate followed. 'Why should we be made responsible for solving world poverty?' one Whitehall purchaser asked. 'My job is to get the best value on behalf of UK taxpayers, not to make sure that people in Africa are properly fed. If the government wants to tackle social issues, it should do that through the democratic process by taking action and passing legislation. It shouldn't pass the buck to us. It's not our job.'

That's a powerful point of view. Why should purchasing professionals be expected any more than anyone else to promote a social agenda?

A prominent business leader put it even more forcefully from industry's point of view. Business, he said, is supposed to make a profit: it's the basis on which a health economy depends. Everything else is secondary, and if business people start getting mixed up with social objectives, the economy will suffer and everyone will be worse off.

The opposing view, put to the Whitehall mandarins by others at the seminar, is that purchasers have more power than most other professionals to influence the way in which people outside their buying organization are treated, and that they should use that power responsibly. The way orders are placed, the conditions attached to them and the price paid for goods and services directly affect those who produce them.

This is not merely an issue involving children sewing footballs for poverty wages in the Far East. Buying organizations – in the public, private and voluntary sectors – can also affect their local economies. For example, councils prioritizing spending in their immediate area can help small businesses and reduce local unemployment. But is that more important than achieving best value for money on behalf of council taxpayers?

Such a policy only reduces total unemployment if the local supplier is less efficient than the non-local. If a small firm has its office in the immediate locality but employs illegal immigrants on meagre wages to fulfil a cleaning contract, it may be far more ethical to give the work to that multinational that employs local staff and pays decent wages.

The crucial factor is that any demands on purchasing professionals to promote social objectives should be made explicit. Then customers, shareholders, taxpayers, politicians, the local community and everyone else know that the professional buyers are not simply going for the lowest possible price but are consciously taking other factors into account on their behalf.

This is a continuing debate in which, for example, the government has promoted the idea of supporting local business. The technical problem is to square this with EU legislation that prohibits geographical discrimination in favour of suppliers.

The practical approach is to avoid positive discrimination but to try to make sure that local firms are given the means to bid for contracts on a par with better-equipped competitors, through such techniques as 'meet the buyers' forums.

Avoiding danger

It may seem rather difficult to be continually trying to avoid doing the wrong thing, but there are some simple guidelines you can follow to avoid hot water. There are often no clear black-and-white answers to some of the real situations in which we may find ourselves. But it is crucial to make sure that the ethical dimension is taken into account and that the rationale for making a particular decision is defensible.

Be open

Make sure that all gifts are out in the open. One senior purchaser told how a supplier offered her a luxury car. She transferred the call to a speakerphone in the open office and asked the supplier to repeat the offer. She then refused it, hung up, and never dealt with the supplier again. That way, she was above suspicion.

Some employers – especially in the public sector – impose strict limits on the value of gifts that can be accepted. Anything above the value of, say, £50 must be openly declared in a register of interests, as MPs now have to do following the 'cash for questions' and other scandals in the 1990s.

Be honest

Don't try to cover up your mistakes: admit to them and be honest about how they happened. Otherwise, you run the risk of creating a façade of lies as your situation becomes ever more complicated.

Ask what others would think

It's easy to rationalize a bad decision by saying that it doesn't really matter or doesn't affect anyone. But think about that carefully. If you were called in by your boss or the managing director, would you be perfectly comfortable explaining what you did and why?

Leave an audit trail

You can't consult your colleagues or your boss every time you have to make a difficult decision. But you can make sure to cover yourself by keeping some sort of record of what you did and why. Probably the easiest way to do this nowadays is to send an e-mail to your boss informing him or her of your decision and briefly adding words to the effect of 'hope that's OK with you'.

The key point, again, is to make sure that others are involved. There is no point in keeping a 'hospitality record book', for example, which is filled in after the event and which no one ever looks at.

In the case of a really difficult situation, it may be necessary to ask for a meeting so that everything can be considered, and then making a note of what was decided.

Don't pass the buck

On the other hand, don't try to transfer responsibility for your decisions on to someone else. As a professional, it's up to you to take responsibility. Saying 'X approved of this, so blame them' may work on occasion, but it's a dangerous strategy if only because X will not take kindly to it. Better to stand up and be counted, for better or worse.

Ask 'what's in it for me?'

If the answer is that there is some personal gain involved in a decision, ask whether that has affected your judgement. It is, of course, very easy to answer 'no'. So you are not the best judge. Ask someone else whom you trust and respect what they think.

A professional code

It's quite common for companies and other organizations to have their own code of ethics or professional conduct. This is usually a fairly simple statement of basic principles that employees are expected to follow. It can be extremely effective, especially if some practical examples of what is acceptable and unacceptable behaviour are given to back up the general principles. But like mission statements, there is the danger that these state the inarguable: 'All employees are expected to adhere to the highest ethical standards.' Such bland exhortations are likely to be of little use in a real dispute between a member of staff and their boss over a dubious instruction.

More value to the individual employee can probably be gained from a code of ethics set out by a professional association. By its nature this will put objective considerations above purely local, tactical pressures.

A professional code can act as a guide for the unwary purchaser and as a court of appeal in any dispute over what is ethical and what is not. It gives the individual professional a bigger framework within which to operate and some form of backing if things go wrong. In more developed professions – notably, for example, in medicine – following the ethical code is well established as a more powerful imperative than obeying managers or employers.

In the UK the Chartered Institute of Purchasing and Supply has produced a code setting out the responsibilities and duties of the professional purchaser (Figure 11.1).

Stakeholders

There are often competing claims on an individual purchaser. There is the immediate employer who is likely to have immediate demands. There are colleagues with particular views and customs to consider. Business partners, suppliers and associates will all have their own perspectives. It's often a question of weighing the claims of various parties or 'stakeholders'.

There are very few easy answers to real moral dilemmas. It's a question of balancing the various competing pressures to your own satisfaction.

Some thoughts on the introductory scenarios

Nothing but the truth

Something akin to the principle of 'buyer beware' applies here – 'seller beware', perhaps. It's not up to someone selling a used car to describe every fault it suffers from, it's up to the buyer to check it out properly

Introduction

1. Members of the Institute undertake to work to exceed the expectations of the following Code and will regard the Code as the basis of best conduct in the Purchasing and Supply profession.
2. Members should seek the commitment of their employer to the Code and seek to achieve widespread acceptance of it amongst their fellow employees.
3. Members should raise any matter of concern of an ethical nature with their immediate supervisor or another senior colleague if appropriate, irrespective of whether it is explicitly addressed in the Code.

Principles

4. Members shall always seek to uphold and enhance the standing of the Purchasing and Supply profession and will always act professionally and selflessly by:
    a. maintaining the highest possible standard of integrity in all their business relationships both inside and outside the organisations where they work;
    b. rejecting any business practice which might reasonably be deemed improper and never using their authority for personal gain;
    c. enhancing the proficiency and stature of the profession by acquiring and maintaining current technical knowledge and the highest standards of ethical behaviour;
    d. fostering the highest possible standards of professional competence amongst those for whom they are responsible;
    e. optimizing the use of resources which they influence and for which they are responsible to provide the maximum benefit to their employing organisation;
    f. complying both with the letter and the spirit of:
        i. the law of the country in which they practise;
        ii. Institute guidance on professional practice;
        iii. contractual obligations.
5. Members should never allow themselves to be deflected from these principles.

Guidance

6. In applying these principles, members should follow the guidance set out below:
    a. Declaration of interest – Any personal interest which may affect or be seen by others to affect a member's impartiality in any matter relevant to his or her duties should be declared.
    b. Confidentiality and accuracy of information – The confidentiality of information received in the course of duty should be respected and should never be used for personal gain. Information given in the course of duty should be honest and clear.
    c. Competition – The nature and length of contracts and business relationships with suppliers can vary according to circumstances. These should always be constructed to ensure deliverables and benefits. Arrangements which might in the long term prevent the effective operation of fair competition should be avoided.
    d. Business gifts – Business gifts, other than items of very small intrinsic value such as business diaries or calendars, should not be accepted.
    e. Hospitality – The recipient should not allow him or herself to be influenced or be perceived by others to have been influenced in making a business decision as a consequence of accepting hospitality. The frequency and scale of hospitality accepted should be managed openly and with care and should not be greater than the member's employer is able to reciprocate.

Decisions and Advice

7. When it is not easy to decide between what is and is not acceptable, advice should be sought from the member's supervisor, another senior colleague or the Institute as appropriate. Advice on any aspect of the Code is available from the Institute.

Figure 11.1 The Chartered Institute of Purchasing and Supply Professional Code of Ethics. Reproduced with permission of CIPS.

before handing over the cash. In this case, it's up to the supplier to ask relevant searching questions about the projected life of the contract and then negotiate accordingly to reach a deal satisfactory to both sides taking all the circumstances into account. It would not, of course, be ethical for the purchaser to lie if asked.

A bribe by any other name

Such payments are, despite attempts to put an end to them, still prevalent in many parts of the world. They are often clearly corrupt. But this could be a clear case of the lesser of two evils: if refusing to go along with the request will deprive people at home of jobs and a foreign competitor is certain to step in and snatch the contract if you don't, it may be necessary to comply with the conditions attached, while not forgetting that such behaviour may be illegal and contrary to professional codes of conduct. The individual purchaser isn't in a position to change working practices around the globe. This must be part of longer-term political and business initiatives in which purchasers can play an important part.

Sheer exploitation

Sacking the supplier will not solve the problem and only creates new ones. The enlightened view of child labour nowadays is not to try and ban it outright but to accept that it plays a major role in some economies and try to work towards change. This should include, for example, making sure that under-age workers spend some of their time in formal education. It is better to work with the supplier, in conjunction perhaps with a respected non-governmental agency, to improve conditions for the workforce and provide community facilities.

It's in the air

What is needed here is an effective company-wide policy. It's in no one's interests for issues like this to be left to informal, personal decision making. As part of their professional role, purchasers should push for such benefits to be incorporated into official company policy one way or another in an above-board way, whether they remain as individual 'rewards' or are ploughed back into the organization as a whole.

French leave

This is a case where the goodies on offer are clearly meant to influence your thinking and it's very difficult to see how you can accept. It just doesn't look good, however you try to rationalize it. If you want a break in the South of France, pay for yourself like everyone else and sleep easy at night.

Mixing business with pleasure

There is a very fine line between playing a round of golf with your colleagues as a kind of professional development and skiving. It's impossible to spell out precisely where that line is, but you'll know it when you see it. Make certain that your colleagues know what you are doing and are aware of the benefits you gain from it. Ask yourself honestly if you are happy with the way you are spending your working time.

12
The Future

Times are changing fast and purchasing won't stand still. In 10 or 20 years the typical purchasing department could be organized along very different lines.

The function of purchasing is expanding and becoming better understood all the time and this is likely to lead in some very interesting directions. Purchasers as individuals have enormous opportunities ahead if they know how to capitalize on their skills and knowledge. They only need to be aware what to look out for and what to avoid.

A changing role

In the past many purchasers occupied a very narrow role concerned solely with buying items and dealing with the associated paperwork. Now the purchasing professional is increasingly expected to see the bigger picture, as we have stressed in this book.

They will be encouraged to gain knowledge of other functions such as sales and marketing, finance and HR. Purchasers will need to be conversant with all aspects of the businesses in which they are employed, as well as with the bigger economic and political scene.

But at the same time, many purchasers are likely to become more specialist, focusing on, for example, particular categories or specific areas of expertise such as writing contracts or overseeing outsourced operations.

The division of labour within the broad purchasing and supply management function is likely to continue going both ways: many purchasers will take on more specialized roles, while at the same time others will become more generalist.

The superpurchaser

Purchasers are concerned with ways of acquiring goods and services, price, value and relations between their own organization and others. It's a much broader role than, say, sales, where the main imperative is to sell as much as possible at the highest achievable price. Signs are already appearing to suggest that purchasing is developing into a bigger function whose concerns are not narrowly limited to the acquisition of goods and services.

Purchasers – the best ones, at least – are experts on negotiating. They have to deal effectively with people outside their organization from a range of commercial operations: their suppliers. They also have to know how to be suppliers themselves when dealing with their internal customers: people in other parts of their organization who make use of their expertise.

Good purchasers require commercial skills. They need to know how to play the market and arrive at a price acceptable to both sides in a deal. They need to know about different methods of acquiring goods and services and drawing up contracts that will make arrangements work effectively. The truly competent purchasing professional is an expert in all the key business skills and should be able to advise others who deal with outside organizations.

It seems certain that the pressure on purchasers to become more expert in all areas of business will intensify in the years ahead. Organizations are recognizing the importance of the purchasing function. They are also recognizing that their purchasing people need to be experts.

General levels of competence within the purchasing community are likely to rise, both by means of training and through a process in which the best people are encouraged and promoted through the ranks. A culture in which there are few real stars will change. It will give way to a more dynamic, meritocratic culture in which the stars are recognized and regarded as role models for others to follow.

The number of people from purchasing backgrounds at top management level is still woefully low. But there is no logical reason for this. Purchasing people fulfil a crucial role within organizations. They can rise to the top as quickly as anyone else given the right motivation and incentives, and this is likely to happen in the years ahead.

How to get to the top

Making it to board level requires certain skills and knowledge. More fundamentally, it requires confidence and a clear understanding of what kind of role an individual needs to play to progress within an organization. It means the ability to see the bigger picture and work within the organization's objectives. It means adopting a strategic approach.

Strategic is a buzzword much used to describe something bigger, more important and impressive than the average. Being strategic sounds hard to achieve. What it really means is actually quite simple, and purchasing professionals can easily put themselves on the road towards being truly strategic players. In practical terms, it means becoming aware of an organization's objectives and the thinking of its management.

At the same time, a pragmatic ability to match desired outcomes with ways of achieving them, making full use of opportunities as they arise, and the ability to spot gaps in an organization's internal market are all useful tools for the aspiring corporate star.

More important than any of these is the ability to tap into the resources held by other people.

It's all about people

The crusade for e-enablement has been a diversion for purchasing professionals in the last few years. Now that it has subsided they can get back to the real job at hand.

It is certainly true that how purchasers make use of the Internet will be a key factor in the future. They need to be able to make full use of the benefits it offers, but also to help their organizations steer clear of wasteful and potentially disastrous deals with IT services providers.

The Internet has brought enormous advances in purchasing as in other areas of business. Huge volumes of information can now be sent around the world at the touch of a computer key. That is making many time-consuming activities redundant.

Nevertheless, the e-revolution has failed to live up to some of the wilder predictions of its early evangelists. E-marketplaces, for example, have largely failed to flourish, for the simple reason that buyers and suppliers are unwilling to sign up to them. The advantages of trading online in a marketplace with your competitors and a range of suppliers simply don't stack up. The technocrats who thought up the idea of the e-marketplace had failed to take account of the psychology of the proposed users.

Other Internet-based operations such as e-auctions have gained a place in the purchasing toolbox, but have not turned out to be problem free. In the construction industry, a sector in which e-auctions might have found an ideal fit, there is persistent resistance.

The government has pinned huge stakes on saving significant amounts of money largely through e-enablement in the public sector. The savings will be pushed into front-line services in health, education and other areas. But signs are starting to emerge that the expectations of what the Internet could offer in terms of savings have been much too high. This will help put the role of procurement professionals very much under the spotlight, even if only as a voice of caution.

Those who are pushing for e-enablement have failed to take human psychology into account. Such tools are expensive and the benefits uncertain. They depend very much on being able to organize processes efficiently, which is something that should be done whether or not e-enablement is due to take place.

Some areas of e-commerce are certain to continue developing. Simple e-procurement – the transactional side of purchasing that speeds up processes that otherwise are laborious and liable to human error – is undeniably a potential benefit if handled properly.

In the wider world, e-mail has been universally accepted as an excellent form of communication. Only the eccentric would argue that it should not be allowed to replace paper for simple day-to-day exchanges. But there are no signs that it will replace paper-based communication altogether. Just as the paperless office and the four-day week have failed to appear, confounding the predictions of the more enthusiastic technophiles, so the Internet has made little real difference to the way people relate to one another.

The ability to interact effectively with other people lies at the heart of all business and nowhere more so than in purchasing. Negotiating, dealing with suppliers and managing internal customers are all areas demanding a high level of people skills. Those who can excel in these activities will be the new stars.

A bigger footprint

Just as the job of purchasing will expand, so will its influence within organizations. Where once purchasers dealt mainly with buying parts and raw materials, now they are increasingly likely to be called on to help with hiring temporary staff, for example, contracting consultants or finding the best deal on a telephone enquiries service.

The purchasing footprint is getting bigger. Purchasers at mobile telephone specialists Vodafone, for example, say that they now influence all aspects of spending except the purchase of handsets, which is still done by engineers.

This means that purchasing will have bigger responsibilities for the procurement of everything from office supplies to temporary staff to IT systems. This will require hugely expanded expertise for many purchasers. Enlarging the purchasing footprint will require more understanding of how the purchaser's organization works and of the wider marketplace outside. Purchasers who know about the economy, markets and the corporate world will succeed.

Purchasing professionals will need to become experts on everything their organization does. Some are already in that position.

The customer comes first

It's not only the way in which purchasers see themselves that will affect their future role. The world in which they work will change too. The make-up of the commercial world and the nature of the supply market will mean new ways of thinking.

A revolution has been taking place in the last two or three decades in the way organizations see themselves, moving away from a provider-first to a customer-first mentality. This is particularly obvious in the public sector, where institutions such as local authorities and the NHS have largely left behind – although it's arguable that there is still a very long way to go – the idea that they exist to provide work for their employees, in favour of one where they see themselves as under a duty to put their customers first. A similar fundamental shift in thinking has also by and large taken place in the private sector. Organizations of all kinds are increasingly being forced by the marketplace to ask what the customer wants and attempt to provide it.

This has happened partly in response to an increasingly sophisticated and demanding public. People nowadays are far less prepared to be fobbed off with second best by employees or organizations who don't appear to take them seriously. Customers want to be treated like individuals and expect their particular demands to be met.

That has brought with it extra pressures on organizations to come up with the goods that people want. Consequently, supply chains are required to respond to individualized demands. Today's economy is increasingly characterized by customization and fragmentation.

Thus the purchasing or supply manager has the ultimate objective of helping make sure that goods get to the market as quickly as possible and that costs along the way are kept to a minimum, so that the final price is as low as possible and customers get what they want.

Most purchasing professionals have little or no responsibility for the wider supply chain. They deal with their immediate suppliers and are not required to look further down the chain to second- and third-tier suppliers and beyond. However, that is increasingly no longer the case.

Changing supply chains

The understanding of how organizations relate to one another is shifting. Where once the concept of the supply chain was widely accepted, now it is being questioned. At the same time the importance of key supply issues is being affected by altering conditions.

The idea of 'lean' supply chains, with the emphasis on reducing stocks and relying on 'just-in-time' techniques, is being called into question by proponents of the 'agile' approach, which they claim takes more account of increasing customer sophistication. A more flexible approach, not so concerned with reducing inventory levels and more responsive to a fragmented and demanding customer base, will become increasingly appropriate.

This debate is part of the environment in which purchasing people work and they need not only understand what is being said, but take part in the discussion themselves. As purchasing becomes a bigger, more strategic function, this is likely to happen. Purchasing professionals will increasingly be able to comment on the wider implications of supply chain issues as they arise within industries and in the media.

Price fixation will fade

An increasingly sophisticated and affluent consumer base is already placing less emphasis on price as the key factor in their purchasing. Quality, service and brand value are becoming more important, particularly among younger generations. Getting exactly what you want when you want it, and with the right label on it, is more important than how much cash you have to hand over. Just look at the booming markets in, for example, trainers or soft drinks and snacks.

Growing public concern over ethical supply chains will feed the same tendency to reduce the importance of price. Increasing numbers of people are prepared to pay more for their goods if they know they have been produced by reasonably paid workers in good conditions rather than by children in sweatshops.

The effect will inevitably filter through supply chains and purchasers will be expected in turn to concern themselves less with price than with delivering the right goods at the right time and to acceptable ethical standards.

Speaking out

Purchasers have an opportunity – some would say a duty– to speak out on various issues that they know something about: globalization, ethical supply chains, achieving value for money and so on. Yet the voice of purchasing is still noticeable largely by its absence in the newspapers and over the airwaves.

The rising importance of the purchasing function will create pressure for purchasers to join public debates on a wide range of topics. Purchasing needs to find its voice alongside the ranks of experts who comment daily on topical issues.

Purchasing and supply management issues are often key to many of the big stories hitting the headlines. The BSE outbreak, for example, involved questions about the long supply chains that had developed for the transport of cattle between farms, directly stemming from a government decision to reduce the number of slaughterhouses on health and safety grounds. The fuel crisis of 2002 also invoked important supply concerns. There were clear issues in these dramatic events in which purchasing and supply management professionals could become involved. Continuing international tension raises a range of supply management issues.

There appears to be growing concern over what could happen if various crises, such as a breakdown in energy supply, were to occur. Such scenarios raise serious purchasing and supply management questions. There are huge opportunities for purchasing and supply management professionals to get involved in such debates.

Looking both ways

The purchasing role is becoming more multidimensional. Traditionally purchasers have been concerned only with the 'upstream' direction in the supply chain: the buying in of goods and services. These purchases then travel, in some sense or another, along the internal supply chain and emerge through sales. They are finally transferred 'downstream' either to another organization in the supply chain or out into the consumer marketplace.

However, in a growing number of organizations purchasers are being involved not merely in the upstream function but its downstream counterpart too. They are being asked to advise sales people on how to deal with purchasers in other organizations. Purchasers are, after all, those most likely to know how their colleagues in other organizations will tend to behave.

It's a short step from there to purchasers moving into a role in which they work closely with sales dealing with both ends of the internal supply chain: the buying in of goods and services and their disposal through the sales function.

This in turn raises the prospect of purchasing ceasing to be a function in its own right. Instead, it is not hard to imagine it merging with sales to become something like a 'supply chain management' function.

This would be the logical extension of the move away from pure purchasing to supply management that is already underway. Purchasing in itself is a fairly narrow activity. Supply management is a much broader concept. The purchasing/sales department of the future goes one step further into a realm where the distinction between the two is blurred.

There are still likely to be specialists in both areas, because purchasing and sales are different kinds of activity. So a merged department will be likely to include people who are predominantly purchasers and others who concentrate mainly on selling.

Nevertheless, the top management of such a department is likely to be someone with purchasing and sales experience who can ensure that the two functions are working seamlessly together. The head of department will not be an expert purchaser or sales person but both.

The purchasing profession

The long ascent of the career purchaser is underway. Once a lowly clerk concerned with little more than administration, the purchaser is now joining the ranks of top business executives. Recruitment specialists report that high-level purchasing skills are much in demand. Salary surveys show that senior purchasing professionals are increasingly generously rewarded for their expertise. The function is more and more recognized in business and among the general public for what it can do, not just by saving money and helping organizations become more profitable, but by offering expert input into the big debates over issues such as e-commerce, globalization and ethical supply chains.

At the same time, purchasing is carving out a place for itself as a profession. In the UK and other countries it has its own institutes with rules, membership conditions, training programmes, qualifications and professional ethical codes.

The definition of a profession has always been debatable, but certain key characteristics are understood. A profession is made up of people with broadly similar expertise. They value good practice and their loyalty is to agreed standards within the profession. A logical extension to these basic characteristics is that a profession will seek to restrict entry to its ranks to those who are able to satisfy the basic conditions.

Many purchasers, though, are emerging from their traditionally restricted bunkers into the wider world of business. They are being encouraged to do so by employers who want them to play a bigger role. Purchasers need to talk to others in their organizations. In particular, for the reasons outlined above, they need to forge links with sales people.

Purchasing certainly involves a specific skill set. But in many ways there is a large overlap with the kinds of expertise found in other commercial functions such as marketing and sales. All these functions require entrepreneurial flair, good market knowledge and excellent interpersonal skills. All can learn from one another.

Pushing for the development of purchasing as a separate profession may give purchasers pride in their status and confidence to deal with their colleagues on an equal footing. But there is also a risk that it could at the same time hold back their development as commercially minded business people.

It seems clear that what is needed is greater cross-fertilization between the commercial functions, not the building of barriers between them. The 'silo mentality' is a phenomenon often observed in all functions, including purchasing. Just how far the promotion of purchasing as a distinct profession will help counter such isolationism is open to question.

There are two broad options: purchasers can continue attempting to section themselves off as a separate profession with its own entry criteria and putting great emphasis on their own standards and interests. Or they can take the view that they have interests in common with other commercial functions such as sales and marketing. That would mean lowering the professional drawbridge and adopting an open and flexible concept of their status.

Final thoughts

Purchasers will change and develop in the years ahead and their prospects are good. People who deal with purchasers will also need to understand that the role is changing and alter their demands accordingly.

The idea that purchasers are the experts in knocking down prices and little else must go. They are capable of far more than that. Organizations should try to maximize the potential of their purchasing professionals. In that way purchasers will gain as individuals and organizations will add value.

It's a win–win situation.

Index